D0208460

★

CONCERNING MUSIC

★

WILHELM FURTWANGLER

WILHELM FURTWÄNGLER

★

CONCERNING
MUSIC

★

translated from the German

by L. J. LAWRENCE

GREENWOOD PRESS, PUBLISHERS
WESTPORT, CONNECTICUT

Library of Congress Cataloging in Publication Data

Furtwängler, Wilhelm, 1886-1954.
    Concerning music.

    Translation of Gespräche über Musik.
    Reprint of the 1953 ed. published by Boosey & Hawkes,
London, New York.
    1. Music. I. Title.
[ML64.F812 1977]   780   76-57174
ISBN 0-8371-8665-X

This edition originally published in 1953 by Boosey & Hawkes,
Limited, London.

Reprinted with the permission of Boosey and Hawkes, Inc.

Reprinted in 1977 by Greenwood Press,
A division of Congressional Information Service, Inc.
88 Post Road West, Westport, Connecticut 06881

Library of Congress catalog card number 76-57174
ISBN 0-8371-8665-X

Printed in the United States of America

10 9 8 7 6 5 4 3

CONTENTS

FOREWORD TO THE FIRST EDITION
(Atlantis-Verlag)

THIS work derives from a manuscript written ten years ago, the earlier publication of which was prevented by a series of internal and external obstructions. The original editor Walter Abendroth, at whose suggestion they came into being, says of the first six conversations:

"These conversations are quite genuine. They took place in Furtwängler's Potsdam home. In addition to the author and the editor, Dr. Furtwängler's colleague Freda von Rechenberg was also present. The theme of each conversation was always agreed beforehand, and she kept the record. Later revision has brought about few alterations from the original. The questions and openings provided by the editor were designed to give the clearest possible run to the dominant train of thought, and to be severely restricted in order not to break the thread once it had been woven.

"The general scope of the conversations was intended to reveal the many-sided experiences and mature reflections of a front rank artist with a universal outlook on the questions and problems of his art, to which he was anxious to give the widest currency in the most useful way. Thus, they afford a glimpse into the artist's private workshop; a glimpse that will interest, will enrich, will grip even those who, while they may have already experienced the living artistic achievements of this personality, have possibly never given much thought to the fact that significant results in the arts do not stem only from given talents, from the sphere of the subconscious, of the impulses, of the temperament, but just as much also from the conscious clarity of the artist's perceptions, from spiritual awareness and from the participation of a discriminating intellect. The reader will no doubt observe with particular interest how much this conscious, reflective contribution has its roots in the work of art itself, which is its starting point."

Dr. Furtwängler has added a concluding seventh chapter to the six orginal ones in which he frankly states his beliefs about the music of the present.

1948

CHAPTER I

A: I noticed you in the audience yesterday at the concert given by your colleague, Mr. X. Surely, that does not often happen!

F: I am beginning to do things just now that for a long time past I could not think of. I enjoy going to concerts and letting music exercise its power over me. I also gain thereby as an artist. I can consider my activities as a conductor objectively and from the outside, so to speak, and take a number of things into account better than if I were myself involved—even if it is often only to learn how not to do it.

A: I can imagine that such was the case yesterday. Or did you approve of the enthusiastic applause of the audience?

F: Not at all, although I can understand it: an effect had undoubtedly been created, even if it was not exactly the effect that the character of the piece demanded. They were so to speak "spurious" effects, put into the work from the outside, that we were given yesterday. But they *were* effects. Whether an effect is spurious or not spurious—that is to say, in a deeper sense, true or untrue—is something the public cannot judge. Every audience—and that includes especially our Berlin audiences, since they are typically metropolitan—must be considered in the first place as a mass without a will of its own, reacting in an uninhibited way, automatically so to speak, to every stimulus. Its first reaction may be true, but it may often be fundamentally false. Further, a first reaction of this sort depends so much on the particular circumstances of the moment that it may quickly become incomprehensible to those very people— the audience itself—who experienced it. How, for instance, does it come about that not only absolute music, but even operas which in subsequent history have proved the most persistent and enduring successes—a *Carmen*, an *Aida* a *Bohème* and so on, fell flat at their first performance?

A : No completely satisfactory answer has ever been given to that question as far as I know.

F : Quite right, the reason is that with audiences everything happens instinctively, incalculably, without complete consciousness. As far as music is concerned, there is nothing about which the so called "public" knows less than about its own mind. Above all, there is one prior condition needful to the listener—whether as an individual or as an audience—if he is to formulate a judgment of real value : and that is, he must have enough *time*. It takes time really to get to know a work, especially in the case of absolute music. How long this learning process takes, this clarifying one's own mind about a work or a composer, it is hard to forecast. It can sometimes take decades. It can even take a lifetime. Remember Bach, remember Beethoven's last works ; remember, too, phenomena such as Bruckner.

Certainly there is another consideration : in many of these cases much of the blame may rest with bad performances, but quality of performance is always the third, the least known factor that must be taken into account in experiencing music. Music is for ever dependent on interpreters. It cannot, like a plastic art, display itself, and clearly the fate of a work hitherto unknown to the listener depends in the first place largely on the performer—the singer, the conductor and so on. It must be rarely that in such circumstances an interpretation makes a bad work seem better than it is—against which the opposite, namely that a good work gets damaged by a bad performance, is an everyday occurrence. But the listener, who is unfamiliar or insufficiently familiar with the piece, cannot possibly be expected to determine whether the absence of effect is due to the work or to the performer.

A : The management of the Berlin Philharmonic recently published a list of works which had proved to be special favourites, "box office draws," with Berlin concert audiences: Interesting conclusions can be drawn from this concerning the psychology of audiences.

F: I know what you are driving at: the story of the "draws" which the public—lazy as in fact it is—wants to hear again and again; the complaint about its unwillingness, if not its inability, to get down to the study of new works and so on. But how, I ask, do you explain the fact that quality always wins in the long run, irresistibly, consistently, with mysterious infallibility? What determines the judgment of "history" which we have come to consider as the highest court of appeal?

As far as the "favourites" of concert audiences are concerned—according to the statistics published by the Berlin Philharmonic they include for example Beethoven's "odd number" symphonies, Schubert's Unfinished, certain Tchaikovsky symphonies, etc.—the preference may be partly based on practical grounds. These works are distinguished by great clarity and lucidity of structure, by a moulding of the ideas which cannot be completely effaced even by inadequate and imprecise performances. They do not depend to the same extent upon the quality of the performance, nor are they as easily spoilt by incompetent performers as are other works of great composers which may be less popular, but are not, for that reason, inferior. Much more interesting to my mind than the question why these works occupy such a preferred place in public favour is another question: why do they keep this place so long and so uninterruptedly? Why do not their effects, apparently achieved by such simple means, in the course of time wear thin? There are many compositions which were "effective" once —perhaps even more effective at the time than those mentioned above—but have since faded into obscurity, or disappeared entirely. And the curious thing is that this would seem to apply particularly to those works which were most blatantly written for effect. Take for example the compositions of that great virtuoso, Liszt, or certain pieces by Berlioz, Wagner, Strauss, Tchaikovsky etc. But then, effect as such and lasting effect are not necessarily identical. Yes, it even looks as if an over big, over conscious effect at the time may stand in the way of, or actually make impossible, that deeper, lasting effect.

Have you not also often noticed in life how one can succumb to an effect and yet—in the same breath—realise how little worth it has. The reaction of an audience will somehow always be commensurate with the effect created, precisely because it is subconscious. Thus there are works that release noisy and vociferous, yet meaningless and empty, applause: it echoes their own emptiness. And there are others to which the audience reacts less spontaneously, yet whose worth is not only immeasurably greater but their effect immeasurably deeper. It is definitely wrong to draw conclusions from the effect made on an audience, i.e., from the volume of the applause, as to the real strength of the impression made by a work, let alone as to its quality. The audience itself—this curious something—does not know how and why it reacts; it reacts automatically and subconsciously, more or less like a barometer. What matters is that one should know how to read this barometer aright and how to interpret that reading.

This the audience itself cannot do. To such an extent is it incapable of doing so, that the individual listener, even the very intelligent listener, has, as I have found hundreds of times, not the slightest idea how he arrives at his opinion. If one asks him, his answer—that is, his conscious judgment —will reflect all kinds of prejudices and associations prominent in his consciousness rather than the real impression made upon him. But it is with the latter alone, and not with the concepts and prejudices peculiar to his limited individuality that he participates in the forming of the real opinion of the audience, which is an involuntary process following definite laws. It is this fact which prompted that theatre expert Dingelstedt to say: "No matter how mistaken the judgment of the individual may be, as a *whole* the audience is damned intelligent."

A: Should it not be one of the tasks of criticism to clarify the audience's conception of itself, and of its own judgments?

F: This the critic cannot do—even if he would like to or thought he could. For he is himself too much part of the audience. There is only one explanation, which I have already given, of the contradiction implied in the fact that the spontaneous reaction of the audience is often wrong, while its lasting judgment is right: the audience must have *time* to arrive at a considered opinion of composer and composition. And this the more so in proportion to how weighty and how difficult of comparison they are. It is by no means unnatural that an audience should at first reject new works. It will, nevertheless, with absolute certainty in the long run fall under the spell of a new composition, *if it is good*.

Let us be clear what this mutual effect of composer and audiences on one another really is. It can only come about through their inter-dependence. Unless the composer realises the dormant potentialities of the audience, unless he tames and bends it to the work, it—and we can easily substitute "nation" for audience in this context—would not even become conscious of itself as such. For in the first place it is just any anonymous crowd of human beings.

Where, for example—to put it paradoxically—would the whole of our concert life be today, if Beethoven had not written his symphonies? It was Beethoven's predecessors and followers, and, above all, he himself, who *created* the concept of a "concert audience" by their works. To be sure, then, this audience is something other than just a formless mass without a will of its own. Suddenly, through the formative influence of these composers, it is possessed of standards. It makes demands. The composer must resist these demands. But he in turn has demands to make on the audience, corresponding to theirs on him. The audience expects such demands from him, for it is these that invest it with its true dignity. There is, after all, a difference between a mass of people welded into a whole by watching a horse race or a boxing match and a crowd made one by listening to a Beethoven symphony. It is the manner of unification which matters.

These differences also exist within the sphere of music. Effects made upon the audience from without are described by Wagner as "sensationalism" which can turn it perhaps into a momentarily intoxicated mass, but cannot make it a true "community". Such sensationalism he laconically defines as "effects without causes". It was precisely in Wagner's time, the dawn of the age of the great virtuosos, that musicians began to strive after these "effects without causes", and to make use of them. Thus, the audience-composer relationship became for the first time the problem it has remained to this day. From that era dates the ever increasing estrangement between the two which today constitutes one of the dangers threatening the whole fabric of our musical life. The craving for effect at any price, which started in the age of Wagner and Liszt, was symptomatic of this estrangement. The exaggeration of effect was in truth an attempt to bridge this estrangement, no less perhaps than today, in quite a different way, the efforts of choral societies, youth clubs and so on are directed to creating the work through the community, instead of, as formerly, the community through the work. The goal is always the same:—the creation of a true "community".

This much is certain: those works alone succeed in turning an audience if only for seconds into a *genuine* community, that take hold of the individual in such a way that he is no longer a separate entity, but a part of his people, a part of humanity, a part of the Divine Nature operating through him. It is only through the medium of such works that an audience ever becomes fully aware of the powers latent in it; and, in spite of their reactions, so aimless and indiscriminate at first sight, it is those works alone that men need and desire. This does not alter the fact that in daily musical life it is to just such works that the audience, as we know from experience, shows the strongest opposition and yields least willingly. In this it is like a woman who wants her happiness forced on her.

A: Do you mean to say the power to impress an audience speaks, if anything, against a work of art?

F: Not at all; that would be a rash and superficial conclusion to draw. To reject Beethoven's works on the grounds that they are effective with the audience would indeed be emptying the baby out with the bath. It is just such a phenomenon as Beethoven that offers the best examples of genuine, of "legitimate", effect. His works make their impression precisely and exclusively because of what they *are*, and not because of what they seem; by their character, and not by their façade. But that Beethoven's effects are what they are is thanks to the clarity with which he says what he has to say. The greatest possible clarity of expression is thus the way—the only way—in which the composer can take into account the existence of the audience. It was Goethe who said: "If a man would tell me anything, he must say it clearly and simply. I have enough within me that is problematic". There is of course a precedent condition: namely, that one should *have* something to say, that is, that one can dare to show oneself naked, without any covering, just as one is. To do so is not for everybody, and those who express themselves in a complicated way— especially if they are artists—may generally have their reasons.

There are works of art which are effective because they set out to be effective. And on the other hand there are those that are effective by their very nature. That is the reason why the impression made diminishes with time in the case of the former but not in that of the latter.

CHAPTER II.

A : Considerable differences of opinion exist between the various performers, e.g., between the conductors of operatic orchestras and symphony orchestras, concerning the degree of difficulty, or even the artistic value, of their work. What do you think about it, speaking as a conductor who is active both in the theatre and in the concert hall?

F : I am fully aware of the fact that conductors of symphony orchestras despise the theatre because of its "slovenliness", its disregard of detail, its lack of precision, whereas conductors of operatic orchestras tend to look upon conductors of symphony orchestras as showmen and charlatans, and hold that the latters' task is considerably easier than their own for the simple reason that a symphony orchestra is less complicated and less subject to the whims of chance. Both are right to a certain extent, and yet they are wrong, because they do not know each other nearly so well as they imagine. However closely related to each other their spheres of activity may seem to be, the fundamental differences between them are such that neither performer is in a position to criticise—and thereby, to pass judgment upon—the other. Even with those conductors who combine both activities in practice, the centre of gravity generally lies on one side or the other. It demands an unusual versatility—a basic requirement in the whole field of interpretative art—to master both equally—and in most cases therefore it is a mistake to put conductors of operatic orchestras in charge of famous orchestral institutions or *vice versa*, only because they happen to be available.

A : Few people seem to realise where the difficulties lie, and what exactly is to be expected of the interpretative musician, who is, after all, the trustee of our most precious music heritage. It happens not infrequently that pianists, conductors etc. master the most difficult tasks brilliantly, only to fall down on apparently quite simple ones.

F: Just so: the question which kind of work is the most difficult of interpretation is by no means irrelevant. For the answer informs us about ourselves as well as about the nature of the work. In this context I should like to tell you a story:

Recently, I spent a few hours in a hotel lounge. The orchestra was playing light music. Although I was with friends, my mind was distracted by the music; as so often before on similar occasions I simply could not help listening, could not help admiring the elegance, the instinctive ease, the subtle fusion of rhythm and sound in the orchestra's performance. Each musician knew his allotted part within the whole. Ardour and sensuousness, too, were not lacking. The programme consisted mainly of pieces from French and Italian operas, with an occasional Strauss waltz, or an arrangement of a piece by Tchaikovsky or Wagner. The final item was Beethoven's *Coriolan* overture, and, lo and behold, gone all of a sudden were the freedom, the verve, the ardour and sensuousness of the performance, gone were all those excellent characteristics that I had just before been admiring in the players. But when I asked them about it afterwards, it appeared that they themselves were not at all conscious of what had happened. They had, they thought, been playing in the "classical style".

For years past I have been coming across various forms of this phenomenon again and again. Take for example that excellent pianist Miss X, who recently played the Tchaikovsky concerto with such natural brilliance and style. She started a few years ago, with Liszt, and today, although she cannot perhaps be said to fulfil all the possibilities of Chopin's F minor concerto, at least she succeeds in conveying a tolerably accurate impression of that autumnal masterpiece. But listen to her playing Beethoven: how inhibited, how positively helpless it sounds—all the brilliance of temperament, sureness of touch and control, no less than the warmth and tenderness of feeling, have suddenly gone out of her playing. All that is left is arid, academic conservatoire standard. The worst of it is that this is by no means an isolated instance: it is the rule nowadays, no matter whether you are dealing with conductors, pianists or any other instrumentalists.

A former colleague of mine once said in the course of conversation that with modern works—by Strauss, Tchaikovsky and so on—one could "give of oneself", whereas it was of course "style" above all that mattered in classical music. Why this "of course"? Are we dealing with an unwritten law here? How often I used to ask myself why classical "style" should be synonymous with boredom. For it is simply not true to say that Tchaikovsky and Verdi demand a greater degree of sensuousness and passion than Beethoven. It is untrue to say that Bach has less "soul" than Puccini. In the case of one the soul is exposed, in the case of the other it is within. That is why in the former it is not only easier to see, but also easier to transmit. It is a matter of proved experience that anyone who can transmit Beethoven—that is, the whole Beethoven, not the "classical-academic emasculated" Beethoven—will always be able to do well with Tchaikovsky and Verdi too, but that anyone who can render Tchaikovsky expressively need not necessarily have the like stature needed for Beethoven and Bach. I think nothing of those who, labelled as Beethoven interpreters, stop short at a Chopin waltz or a Puccini opera.

Of course, there is a problem implicit in all this, about which it is not at all easy to clear one's mind. Perhaps we can express it in biological terms: sensibility, intellect, heart, understanding, all had an equal share in the works of the great classical composers. The separate parts were created with and out of the whole, and the whole with the parts. Notwithstanding the fulfilment in each successive moment, the creative urge (responding to the natural feelings) was, unconsciously, of course, directed to the context as a whole. The impulses were no less elementary, but they were indeed less *exclusively* of the nerves, less *exclusively* emotional in character than was the case with the music of a later age. Development in the nineteenth century was towards the release of ever shorter and apparently—but only apparently—more spontaneous impulses. This made composition not, as was believed, more elementary, but rather more primitive. The musician of today, whether in the hotel lounge or the concert hall, whether he be a violinist or a conductor, is disinclined (if it is not beyond his grasp) actually to respond to the wider context, i.e., to the spiritual experiences from which that context springs. Owing to the turmoil of the world around him, the nature of his training—both at the conservatoire and in practice—and the character of most of the works with which he has to deal, the modern musician is no longer prepared for such a task, nor is he equal to it. Consequently he learns to differentiate between the music with which he can identify himself, living it, creating it, and the other kind, from which—reporting on it, so to speak—he stands aside. And it is performances of this latter sort that he thinks of as having "style". Thus, a Strauss waltz or a piece by Debussy or Tchaikovsky is invariably and in all circumstances nowadays played much better at first than are the works of Bach or Beethoven.

A: Do you not think that all this is a necessary consequence of historical developments?

F: Certainly, in so far as it is the creations of an era which set the standard for the performances in that era. The creative musical tendencies of the age exert considerable influence over the current attitude towards the classical masterpieces. But in this context I should like to say the following: classical music—and by this, I do not mean "classical" in the historical sense of the word (in which case part of the so-called "romantic" period would have to be included), but as a sort of collective term to signify those works on which our concert life is still based, and without which it would in practice not exist—classical music is imbued with a kind of musical *logic*, which, in its way, is no less stern, no less compelling than the logic of a train of argument. Anybody who experiences an adequate performance of such a work immediately and automatically feels it. This "musical logic"—as I should like to call it—pervades the entire *œuvre* of the classical composers. Later, it gradually becomes weaker, thinner, less cogent. When programme music came into fashion, an attempt was made, by means of an artificial logic, imposed from without, to replace the purely musical one, and substitute through the programme, so to speak, an association of a more tangible kind. But at least it was still an association, even if not a purely musical one. It was gradually being discovered—Liszt had started the trend—that the laws of pure music which presupposed a persistent musical elaboration of the whole of the composition, were superfluous, if not actually detrimental, from the point of view of maximum momentary effect. It is sufficient if details are made to stand out in bold relief, and if they in themselves can be called music. No attention at all is paid to the *whole*: that is confidently left to the "programme". Strauss himself was by no means unalive to this. It was of course possible by this means to achieve momentarily greater freedom of movement and to create something new. But at what a price! From the purely musical point of view, music was "put together". What had once been an organism became an "arrangement"—rather like a flower arrangement, this can often be done with a great deal of taste, but it no longer has any connection whatever with the eternal laws of music.

This evolution by which the part came to take the place of the whole, went further with the passage of time, in that the logical units of music into which the whole was thus disintegrated became smaller and smaller. The works of Max Reger—who marks the end of this particular line of development as far as abstract music is concerned—provide the best examples of this dual activity: large-scale arranging on the one hand, and on the other, as it were composition, just from bar to bar, from one fraction of a bar to the next. It is precisely the manner in which Reger renders the smallest details complete in themselves which exemplifies his talent, his lively and supple fancy. But he was only capable on very rare occasions of embracing in one musical structure the minimum required to constitute what the terminology of an earlier age described as a theme. Hence his predilection for writing arrangements of or variations on the themes of other, earlier, composers.

It was only natural that all this should have some influence on the performance of music. By fixing their eyes on detail, musicians became more and more incapable of appreciating its structure, and of taking into consideration the organic relation between the whole and its parts in those works which really constitute a musical whole. This and nothing else is briefly the reason why, on the whole, classical works are given worse performances today than more recent ones.

I am personally convinced that, generally speaking, they are given worse performances than they were, let us say, fifty years ago. Current composition is always the measuring rod: like a barometer, it indicates the spirit of the age. The quality of composition usually determines the quality of performance. The sense of logic and lucidity in music must be exercised, like all the other senses, like every other organ, it must be used and trained constantly. But modern music in general demands of the performer the exact opposite of what earlier generations understood by structure in music. It is just as if one were to refrain intentionally from directly regarding the whole, to abstract oneself as far as possible, in order to seek satisfaction within the framework —for such there must be—of an "arrangement" dictated by the brain. Such pieces are of course infinitely easier to perform than classical works are, since an artist, provided he has the necessary technique, will never find it difficult to convey individual images strikingly. He will be faced with a problem only when he is called upon to integrate several such images into the whole of which they form an organic part, provided of course that such a relationship exists.

We can even go so far as to say that the task increases in difficulty in proportion to the profundity of the level of experience on which this relationship exists. As far as rhythm, harmony, instrumentation and the execution of details are concerned, the demands made upon the performer today may well be more exacting than they were in the past. But as experience repeatedly shows, it seems to be easier to overcome these difficulties than it is to master the more latent, so to speak "intrinsic" difficulties implicit in the mysterious interplay in a classical composition between the parts and the whole. How incomparably more difficult it often is for a conductor to perform a Haydn symphony— that is, if all the verve, sentiment, and high spirits of this music are to be brought out to the full—than to perform the majority of contemporary works.

And yet there is no indication that the present age is at all aware of this fact, witness the apparently complete ignorance of the really wretched way in which classical masterpieces are performed today. Utter confusion seems to reign amongst the public as far as this problem is concerned. People simply do not know what to look for. They talk about "strict adherence to the score", yet listen in silence or actually applaud when the most incredible liberties are taken with it. The *spiritual* problems with which the great classical masterpieces are in fact concerned have long since been relegated to oblivion. In this respect we have lost our critical faculty, we are no longer qualified to judge. In this respect we have imperceptibly become like children, just as the great classical composers may appear "childlike" to us in the light of the latest products of modern rhythm, harmony and polyphony.

But we must realise that there are certain natural limits to the technical, i.e., material difficulties involved in the performance of music, deriving not so much from the stuff of music as from man. A person's technique can of course be improved by training, but only within the limits set by his ability, whereas the material admits of a very much higher degree of development and complexity. Thus a sprinter may attain a high speed by means of thorough training, but what is his speed compared with that of a motor car? The speed with which the car enables me to move admits of far greater increase. Yet it is not I who move faster, but the car. I myself, "the centre of power", remain unchanged. But in art, by which Man expresses himself, he alone is the measure of things. Harmony of course admits of great nicety and infinite complexity. But if it is also to be the expression of a *spiritual experience*, if it is to pierce the heart, as it were, this complexity must not appear complicated. Rhythmical complexities, too, can be considerably increased, but must be kept within natural limits, if they are to play their full and vital functions side by side with the elements of melody and harmony.

In spite of this the musician of today imagines that he is serving the cause of progress when he surrenders to the "demands of the material", when he treats it as it were as an end in itself, when he loses himself in its involutions. As a consequence of this, the emotional coherence of the whole must of course be sacrificed more or less completely. But once things have gone thus far, there is no holding back. No longer kept within limits by a higher authority, the material begins to proliferate. And, since the intellect is now at liberty to expend all its ingenuity upon details, there is a continual increase of complexity. Thereafter not only does each detail bear the stamp of Intellect Unbound—acquiring that character of cold perfection which is somehow felt to be mechanical—but it also ceases to convey any message to the normally emotional listener and tends to appeal only to those listeners whose interest is of a technical and intellectual nature: it becomes spiritually impotent. No sooner is the harmonic line divorced from its support of harmonic and melodic progressions, than it begins to lose its inner meaning. Be there never so many complicated modulations and transitions it fails to appeal to the emotions of the listener. It almost seems as though excessive transitions deprived each other of effect. The same applies to polyphony. Rhythm too, as such, can also be incredibly complicated, but this, likewise, is destroyed if certain basic laws are disregarded. All this show of ingenuity is wasted on the listener; these rhythms become monotonous and tiring, no matter how immeasurably difficult they may be in the first place to the performers.

All this is the fruit of the age of technique in the truest sense of the word. That is why the kind of intelligence required of the performer who would master such technical difficulties is so common nowadays. It is readily acquired in training by anyone with a modicum of talent. The same kind of intelligence required for the servicing, dismantling and repairing of motorcars—in which, so I am told, even the quite primitive peoples are far advanced—enables the musician of today to play from memory the most complicated harmonies and rhythms: memory is mostly mechanical anyway. There is of course some point in playing from memory if it serves to make the artist free of the whole emotional gamut of a work; in all other circumstances, when, as frequently happens nowadays, it is practised as an end in itself, its proper place is in the music-hall.

Let us look for a moment at the great masters. Bach's horizontal melodic line and polyphony appear to be complicated, his harmony relatively complicated, and his rhythm perfectly simple. Beethoven's melodic line and harmony are very much simpler, but his rhythm and therefore the whole structure of his compositions is very much more complex. Wagner, Strauss, Debussy, Strawinsky, each is complex in a different way, that is to say, the relative complexity of one element of composition is counterbalanced by the relative simplicity of another, an inevitable consequence of the fact that man's faculties of apperception are limited. Our ear has not "developed", as many people still believe, with the "development" of music. The sense of hearing has its natural limitations like all the other senses. But the demands made upon the human ear in the course of history have undergone a change. When these demands were particularly exacting in one respect, they had to be reduced in another, if the whole was to remain an expression of spiritual experience. Fundamentally the human soul has never changed.

To sum up, we can only say from the performer's point of view that every art which seeks to represent a totality of experience is difficult, and, as practice repeatedly proves, not infrequently most difficult when it appears most easy. For it is this totality of experience that is often the least obvious. And again, it may be said that every art which, abandoning this human conception of totality, replaces it with details, limited to characterisation alone, with specialised effects, with triumphs of exaggerated virtuosity, is easy—be it what it may: for it no longer has need of the spiritual powers of the whole man as a medium of transmission, but only of the intelligence and the nerves. And these are just what are cheap to come by today. Everything purely mechanistic is a matter of training. But that understanding from which the word Art derives has nothing whatever to do with training.

CHAPTER III.

A: If I understand you aright you consider that modern music is easy, and classical music difficult to perform.

F: I would not express it in such general terms. And I should like to point out that I am not an unconditional panegyrist of "classical" music as such. I am a modern musician, and as such I am interested in this so-called "classical" music only in so far as it appeals to the man of today, in so far, that is, as it is "modern music". I have never been able to take more than a limited interest in the moribund art of a bygone age. But my interest is all the greater in those works which must, from the point of view of practical experience, still be considered as the real pillars of our music life. It cannot be denied that this music is in grave danger today. There are many indications of the fact. It means that the whole of music life as we know it is threatened, and I consider it all the more important to draw attention to this danger since we have as yet scarcely become conscious of it. I would therefore answer your question as follows:

It is not at all easy to say what constitutes the task of the performer (and difficult enough it would seem to be, since it is so seldom well done), because it is of a spiritual rather than of a technical nature. An examination of the history of instrumental technique will show that there are now hardly any technical difficulties still to be overcome. They do not present a problem. But other things have almost imperceptibly begun to become problematical in a way which no one would once have expected. What was naïvely enough admired as technique in former times was not at all what we understand by the term today. It was not the "technique" of a Mozart and Beethoven, or, at a later age, of a Paganini and Liszt, which impressed their contemporaries, but the voice of the man behind this technique, who made it the vehicle of his inner necessity. The problems of interpretation only arose when technique became something which could be divorced from the personality of the artist as a whole, to be attained at any time by training. These problems are not problems of "technique" at all; they are only concerned with the one point at which technique and soul meet.

What are the limits beyond which technique cannot be developed without ceasing to be an expression of spiritual experience, and thus losing its *raison d'être*? That is the decisive question. And of course, in this connection, I can only repeat that, taken as the expression of a spiritual experience, the easiest piece becomes "difficult", and *vice versa*: once the need for spiritual penetration and justification is dispensed with, the most seemingly difficult becomes easy.

But we have seen—and this must be regarded as a special handicap for the performer of the masterpieces of the past —that the manner in which soul and matter are fused differs with individual composers. It varies so much that one and the same method of expression is frequently used for entirely different purposes by different composers. In the music of Bach, for example, every note has at once a harmonic and also a melodic functional meaning. Rhythm does not appear as an independent factor; the whole piece unfolds without convolution or constraint. There is not the slightest suggestion of momentary weakness—the quiet and continual force of the drawing of melodic lines and the development of harmony represent an optimum of flowing existence, a state of permanency harnessed as it were to the course of events (this, by the way, is the ideal of modern man, consciously aiming at hygiene, to whom nothing appears more desirable than the smooth and uninterrupted fulfilment of the vital functions.)

In the case of Mozart—to mention only the main stages —there is no longer any such state of permanency; here already action preponderates. It was Mozart who began to employ those contrasts of rhythm of which Bach did not know or which he deliberately endeavoured to exclude. But with Mozart, too, the whole flows smoothly without convolution or inversion. He is not an epic composer like Bach nor a dramatic composer like Beethoven. He combines both elements in a unique way, never again achieved after him. Whatever he does he does—like a consummate swordsman—with superb ease and mastery; he fulfils great and difficult tasks with all the elegance and charm of a man of the world, without the slightest trace of strain or uncertainty. He is the ideal of the theoreticians, of the teachers of music. Availing himself of the sudden emancipation of rhythm, Haydn, the real father of the "sonata form" was the first to introduce the whirlpools of convolution and inversion into music. To him can be traced back the problems which were later to occupy the attention of Beethoven. Mozart was the more elegant, the more blue-blooded, as it were, of the two. Haydn belonged more to the people; Mozart has greater nobility, greater sweetness, Haydn more fervour, more *joie de vivre*. Who would dare claim that one is greater than the other? Haydn's symphonies and quartets contain the essence of *joie de vivre*. His music is young, younger than that of any of his predecessors or successors. I have never been able to understand why Wagner did not grasp Haydn. The world would be the poorer without him.

But with Haydn, for the first time, the musical unity of the whole work, that great endowment of the period, was no longer spontaneous as in the case of Bach or the still more fortunate Mozart, but had to be striven for. This is, properly speaking, the starting-point of modern music. In Haydn's works, and, to an even greater extent, in Beethoven's, Bach's "being", Mozart's "happening" are turned into "becoming". With Bach, a work comes to an end; Haydn and Beethoven bring it to an end. Thus the achievement of the unity of musical logic, musical action on the one hand and spiritual logic, spiritual action on the other becomes the problem of the age.

There are still people even today who play off Bach against Beethoven, representing Beethoven as a Romantic, a subjective writer, and so as a destroyer of the natural order, an influence to be overcome. This view is engendered by a profound misunderstanding, which is, admittedly, fostered by the manner in which Beethoven's works are usually performed. To compare Bach with Beethoven is like comparing an oak tree with a lion, animal life with the life of a plant.

With Beethoven, music became for the first time capable of expressing what in Nature is the catastrophic element. The catastrophe is no less natural than is the slow organic development of evolution: it is another form of Nature's expression. So far the character of music had been epic, now it gradually became dramatic. In ancient Greece, too, Homer preceded the tragic poets. Such things do not happen by chance. The great epic corresponds to a more primitive stage of development than the drama, which presupposes the possibility of isolating the fates and characters of individuals, of allowing them to develop according to inherent laws. Epic precedes drama because description is the first sort of encounter with reality. Not until reality has been mastered by description does the creative artist acquire the degree of detachment necessary for his characters to develop according to the law inherent in each: not until then can he treat his creatures as though they no longer depended upon him but lived their own lives, fulfilling private destinies.

Bach, of course, achieves certain "tragic" effects—one has only to think of the Passions. But Bach, in spite of this, remains essentially epic; with him, a subject represents an unalterable entity, which, although it is developed, never has a life of its own. The decisive factor which was introduced into the history of music by Haydn and which became a complete reality in Beethoven's work, was that the subject should develop organically within the work, like a Shakespearian character. With Bach, the entire potential development of a work is implicit in the subject as such, in reality he never does anything which is not in accord with his main theme, even when he introduces counter-subjects (e.g., in a fugue). He is monothematic in the real sense of the term. The forms he employs—the fugue, the aria etc.— are all presented to us in the same broad flow. Each piece runs its predestined course with iron consistency. With Beethoven, the course of a piece of music is not prescribed to the same extent, although it would be entirely wrong to say that the degree of cogency in the development of the piece is less than it is with Bach. But with Bethoven this development is not predetermined solely by the first subject; Beethoven uses several subjects from the opposition and permutation of which the piece develops. These different subjects live and develop in interaction. They have to bear a destiny of their own. The work is moulded—to no one else in the whole history of music does this apply to the same extent—into a whole from parts which in themselves often represent the greatest contrasts imaginable.

For some time it was publicly argued—with no less a man than Hans Pfitzner taking part in the debate—that Beethoven's ideas as such had no special virtue: it was what he made of his ideas that mattered. There was one school of thought which rightly held with Pfitzner that intuition must always be the essential factor, even in works such as Beethoven's, which show evidence of much "hard work". The other school of thought—tending for the most part, though without saying so, to make the part played by intuition appear as small as possible because they themselves were intellectuals—represented Beethoven as the typical example of an artist with an infinite capacity for taking pains. It is true that certain of Beethoven's subjects (e.g., the first subject of the *Eroica* or of the fifth symphony) cannot be considered as particularly brilliant. But Beethoven's genius consists in surrounding every subject with an appropriate aura, an appropriate "climate"; and secondly—and this is the most important point—in managing to find for every subject the very companions which enable its possibilities to be developed to the fullest extent. Beethoven's supreme genius, which is unsurpassed in this respect in the history of music, consisted in his ability to invent seemingly within the scope of one and the same overall "mood" several subjects of entirely different individual characteristics which only attain their full development by establishing a living contact with each other, thus forming a new and all-embracing unity which exceeds by far the limitations of the individual themes. It is not, therefore, a genius for the invention of themes that is Beethoven's only characteristic—though in this respect, too, he has something to show (so that those who favour the "hard work" theory are not entirely wrong). His intuition goes far beyond this; at his best he succeeds in finding a whole series of subjects which appear to cling together by fate, one might almost say by a law of nature, and which, in supplementing one another, endow the work with all the fulness and strength of life that their creator has to impart.

This is a method which I call "dramatic" in the real sense of the word. Beethoven's subjects develop in mutual interaction like the characters in a play. In every single subject of every Beethoven work, a destiny is unfolded.

In the "klassische Walpurgisnacht" in *Faust, Part II*, Goethe represents the clash of opinions as personified by two Ionic philosophers: Thales claims that the world was created out of water (i.e., by continuing evolution), Anaxagoras claims that it was created out of fire (i.e., catastrophe). These theories represent two diametrically opposed concepts, obvious archetypes of a possible interpretation of nature. And there really are different kinds of organic development. There is the more feminine, or evolutionary principle, and the catastrophic, which may be called the masculine principle. The latter, too, is part of organic nature—in contrast to everything purely intellectual or mechanical, which operates on an entirely different level of existence.

A : Just now you applied the term "dramatic" to Beethoven, the composer of absolute music. What is the connection between this and the music-drama of an operatic composer like Wagner?

F : Wagner is a poet who pursues his poetic dreams with the aid of music. But he is in a category by himself. As far as Beethoven is concerned, we can say that he succeeds in attaining within the most restricted frame, within the scope of a sonata, the kind of effect which Aristotle ascribes to tragedy. And it is this point which shows in what respect the two arts of music and poetry are related and where they differ. In a tragedy, the catastrophe—the wreck of clashing forces—tears apart and re-fashions those who participate in it, establishing thereby a harmony on a higher plane, that "tragic catharsis" of which Aristotle speaks. If we apply this to the realm of music we find, curiously enough, that music itself is incapable of achieving tragic effects of this kind, and that a real musical tragedy has therefore never been written. A work with a tragic ending can be a music-drama like *Tristan* or *The Twilight of the Gods*, it is the subject, the drama, which is tragic, not the music as such. Attempts have of course been made in this direction from time to time, even in the field of pure music—the most recent of these was made by Tchaikovsky in the *Pathétique*, which has great powers of suggestion, and is deeply rooted in the Slav national character—but their effect is nevertheless very different from that of the great spoken tragedy. Not "tragic catharsis" but gloom, despair, and resignation have the last word. One cannot help feeling that a climax of sorrow and struggle and conflict can only be transitory, because in music the tragic element does not possess the same liberating power as in poetic tragedy: it does not exalt man above his normal condition, but confines him within himself as within a prison. It is by no means accidental that the funeral march is only the second movement of the *Eroica*. The *ultimate* effect of tragedy (a subject on which Goethe and Schiller conducted an extensive correspondence), its liberating effect, its power to save, is released by music—and this shows the profound difference between the two arts—by the opposite of the "tragic element", that is, by *joy*. It is at this point that the essentially dionysiac character of music stands revealed. And no one has shown this more clearly than Beethoven. No matter what the prevailing mood of individual movements may be, every sonata, every string quartet is in its way a drama, not infrequently a real tragedy, whose concentrated ecstasy is altogether beyond the reach of poetry. Richard Wagner realised this. At the point where poetry acquires wings and soars into the grandeur of the superhuman, music will somehow always appear tongue-tied, imprisoned, as it were, within itself. At the point of ecstasy which marks the limit of poetical expression, music only begins to reveal what it is capable of. This abandonment to the dionysiac side of life, to joy, is as alien to Goethe, whose approach is essentially bounded by poetry, as it was to the epic sense and feeling for form of the Greeks—though they, of course, possessed the other as well. This is fundamentally the explanation of Beethoven's great finales in a major key, a monumental example being the finale of the ninth symphony.

A: But surely there are works by Beethoven which are not dramatic in character. For example, is not the reason why Beethoven's so-called "even" symphonies are less popular with the public because they are less dramatic?

F: The character of Beethoven's works is as rich and diversified as Nature herself. But, in calling them dramatic, I was referring not to the "world" or to the "mood" which they express, but to the mode of expression on which they are based; what I said just now about the manner in which the subjects are formulated—the bringing together and integration of entirely disparate elements—in the creative principle by which he works. It informs and permeates all his compositions in the smallest detail as in the whole, in the individual theme as well as in the division of the whole into movements, comparable to the acts of a play. For the profoundly necessary relationship between these movements in their sequence is undeniable. And the sense of the "fruitful contrast", as I should like to call it, which dominated Beethoven, the contrast from which is born a *new* entity, is shown clearly in all his work. There is such tremendous variety in Beethoven's works precisely because it is this synthesis which is aimed at, because every piece consequently has a world of its own to express. This even affects details of form, style, the growth of a composition. No two works by Beethoven are similar in form, whereas, for example, Bruckner's few are as alike as peas in a pod as far as the various elements of form (the codas, for instance) are concerned.

It seems as if Beethoven has been deliberately searching for apparently irreconcilable antitheses. Thus a dramatic and hard movement full of action (first major example, the Kreutzer sonata, last example, sonata op. III) is followed by a set of variations written in the most relaxed and serene musical style imaginable. But it is only the two together that constitute for Beethoven a *whole*.

These sets of variations on a slow theme, especially the ones written during the last years of his life, are, of course, by no means accidental. They are not variations in the usual sense. They presuppose the existence of that type of Beethoven theme which is so balanced in itself, which has its being so completely within itself that the whole great set of variations which follows is as it were no more than an exhalation, an unfolding, an expansion of the theme, with nothing added that does not spring from its own nature. And such a movement—representing the highest degree of relaxation ever dared in music—is then inserted between movements in which tension seems to have been heightened to breaking-point. Think for a moment of the ninth symphony. Consider the theme of the adagio, steeped in an other-worldliness which properly belongs to the sphere of religion: how it expands in the variations which follow, how it is lost in innumerable arabesques—as if a stylistic urge were at work which, in terms of art history, would probably have found expression in the Gothic style: in Beethoven's case not, however, for its own sake, as with the Gothic builders, but rather as a necessary part of an ordained whole. It seems as if the full purpose of the adagio —which in spite of its profoundly contemplative character must remain an episode, part of one uniform creative process—were only revealed in retrospect, when the finale is announced in frightening tones. Nothing is merely strung together, everything is developed organically from what has gone before. Thus was Beethoven enabled not only to write this first movement of the ninth symphony— a world in itself, whose contents and style have formed and overshadowed whole generations of composers—but also to follow it up, as its necessary supplement and contrast, with a scherzo which is the archetype of all large-scale symphonic scherzi; then to represent, in the adagio, the obverse side of the world, here too, as in the preceding movements, going to the limits of human ability; to feel and finally to put all these movements into his very own type of perspective—perspective by means of the last movement, thus revealing in their entirety the tragic and dionysiac possibilities of music. That is creative power indeed!

But I should like to go back for a moment to what you said about the undramatic character of certain works by Beethoven, especially the "even number" symphonies. Of course there are such works; they even outnumber those which are of a more tragic and dramatic nature. Beethoven enjoys an extraordinary wealth of moods. But each of these moods—and this is the point—is expressed with the absence of ambiguity peculiar to him. Each expression is always pursued and exploited to its utmost limitations. Those half-moods of Mozart or the early Romantics, in which the soul itself seems not to know what it wants, are as foreign to Beethoven as are the bourgeois-inspired hesitancy, the inability to "go the whole hog", which are to be found constantly in Schumann and Brahms, or the incapacity to transcend the limitations of the given means that we so often see in more recent music. Especially in his latter period Beethoven frequently expresses spiritual extremes.

But this makes him more difficult for the mass of the public to understand, so that the effect of his music loses in breadth what it gains in depth. A work like the seventh symphony, with its unearthly serenity and its wild gigantic high spirits is, I think, intelligible in its entirety only to the few. This also applies to the sweet idyllic strains of the "pastoral", which Wagner has apostrophised so aptly with the words of Christ: "This day shalt thou be with me in paradise". Long passages of this symphony are imbued with a kind of natural piety, a quality of absorption which is related to the religious sphere and nowadays does not appeal universally either to audiences or performers.

The remarks and prejudices voiced again and again by performers as well as audiences show very clearly to what extent these works, which are after all accessible to the public, are misunderstood: that the eighth symphony is "harmless", that the "pastoral" is "weak", that it has "no end", that the last movement of the ninth is "banal", etc. Beethoven, the great unknown, is a subject which reflects mainly on the inadequacy of our performers.

CHAPTER IV.

A: You have pointed out again and again that it is purely the laws of music which are operative in the great classical masterpieces. This could, you claim, be demonstrated particularly clearly in the works of Beethoven, to pick out a representative example. But there can, I think, be no doubt that Beethoven, quite apart from the laws of music, was inspired in his ideas.

F: I should like to say first, that the word "idea" is merely a description of a kind of process of concentration within the world of *reality*. In this sense there are ideas demanding realisation wherever we have to deal with human beings. Thus, in political life, there are the various ideas on the nature of the state as conceived by nations and creative statesmen; or again, in the sphere of religion, there are the various forms and realisations of religious communion. If a work of art, for example a piece of music, would appear to embody an "idea", this does not make it any the less a piece of music. People who believe that it does have fallen prey to the fallacy which results from attempting to record the idea rationally in words—a task which is, of course, impossible without sacrificing the substance of the idea to a very considerable extent. This kind of rationalised idea should never in any circumstances be placed on an equal level with reality itself. With Beethoven, too, it is not the "ideas" which are of primary importance, but the manner in which they are realised in his music.

Beethoven more than anyone else had an urge to express everything in a purely musical form. This is demonstrated particularly clearly by his attitude towards a given text. No matter how hard he may try, e.g., in parts of *Fidelio*, or in the *Missa solemnis*, to express the meaning of every word in music, he never entirely succeeds in getting away from his purely musical conceptions of form. The sonata form, and, as its simpler prototype, the *Lied*, with its repetitions etc., are, literally speaking, "in his blood", everything is, in the last analysis, somehow related to them, linked up with them. Poet and composer find in him no comfortable half-way house. That is the reason why he could not become a lyricist like Schubert or a music-dramatist like Wagner—not because he was less, but because he was more of a musician, because he was more exclusively a musician; because the postulate of pure music affected him more strongly, more inexorably. The musician in him felt inhibited, not inspired by a text: he would not allow the textual form of a word to dictate to him what form his music should take. Thus Beethoven becomes completely himself only when he is free to follow exclusively the inherent demands of music.

That is the reason why he attempted in most cases to resolve a given text into separate phases which he then tackled purely from the point of view of music, for instance the individual numbers of *Fidelio*, starting with the wonderful quartet—a most profound inspiration on a trifling occasion—and then the movements of the *Missa solemnis*, which can be described in this connection as a symphony with words.

A: This undoubtedly applies to all the works in which Beethoven set words to music. But what about the ninth symphony, when after three purely instrumental movements Beethoven suddenly resorted to words—could not the explanation be found in a non-musical, literary impulse after all? Or is there a purely musical explanation even for this?

F: Of course there is. Moreover it is particularly important to clear the matter up, as ideas about this last movement have tended to be extremely confused ever since Wagner's somewhat arbitrary attempts to interpret it. We find, first of all, that in this instance, as in all others, Beethoven approaches his text purely as a musician. Already

Wagner noticed that the music does not fit the words, but that the words were, not very happily, subsequently fitted to the melody. What really happened was that Beethoven was searching for suitable words to illustrate what he as a musician wanted to say, following the inner sense of the preceding movements—the whole composition—and to complete the work as a whole, and that he happened to find these words in Schiller, with his tendency to embrace the abstract and the ideal. A more realistic poet would perhaps have given preference to one definite manifestation of joy rather than to the idea of joy. But the latter suited Beethoven's purpose exactly: he was not to be nailed down by details of the text nor was he to be restrained in his freedom of musical expression. Thus he culled a few stanzas only from Schiller's poem and incorporated them in his music with repetitions *ad lib*.

Considered purely from the point of view of form, this last movement is cyclic in construction like the adagio which precedes it, or the final movement of the *Eroica*, or hundreds of similar movements by Beethoven: it is a set of variations on a grand scale. Admittedly, the individual variations would seem to have been adapted to the requirements of the text, and there is also a second subject which is heard later in a fugato passage together with the first subject, but the musical character of a set of variations albeit on a grand scale, is preserved to the very end.

A: But the significant thing, surely, is that the human voice should suddenly be introduced for no apparent musical reason. How do you explain that?

F: For a composer like Beethoven, in whose works something "happens", a process of "becoming" is manifested, the last movements must have presented the greatest and hardest problems, since it was in them that the last, the decisive word was spoken. Beethoven attempted to attack this problem in a great many different ways. He could release the tension which had been mounting in the

other movements by means of a finale full of high spirits
and *joie de vivre*—a method in which Haydn had preceded
him. There are many such finales, dating especially from
his middle period. Then there are finales in which ecstatic
merriment is given a diabolical twist, as for example the
final movements of the quartets in C minor and C sharp
minor, or the finale, again in a minor key, of the *Appas-
sionata*. It seems that he had at first intended to write such
a finale for the "ninth"; as we know from his scrapbooks,
he later used the theme of this finale to similar purpose in
the string quartet in A minor, opus 132. Or again, there are
finales which manifest a kind of humorous mastery of the
world and which appear to be superficial although they are
in fact profound. Such final movements are difficult for the
man in the street to understand. Thus the last movement
of the great trio in B flat major, which may appear inferior
to the wonderful adagio which precedes it, in reality represents a liberation, a progression into lighter, purer air.
Then there are rondos, as exemplified for the first time in
the *Sonata Pathétique*, in which the tension of the other
movements is relieved in epic and elegiac strains. With
Beethoven, the possibilities of each final synthesis are as
varied as the works themselves.

What prompted him, in the "ninth", to choose a text,
to use the human voice, was nothing more than an urge
born of the preceding movements, i.e., of purely musical
elements after all. It was the *theme* of this last movement
which brought with it everything else, the text, the human
voice, and the cycle form. This archetype of all themes, an
invention of the *musician* alone in Beethoven, could never
be the explanation or illustration of a definite text. On the
contrary, it is rather the poem which gives the impression
of being an interpretation of the theme. And in the same
way we must consider the use of the human voice as nothing
more than the natural "instrumentation" of this ageless
melody.

The way he uses this "instrument", the way the human voice is introduced as such, yet musically motivated, reveals Beethoven's genius in all its glory. Any other composer would probably have started with the recitative and would then have embarked upon the choral movement. Not so Beethoven, who, recognising nothing but musical necessity within his work, uses the following method of development: first, the adagio is spun out into the infinite. It seems as if he would never be satisfied, as if he could never stop. This sharpens the contrast with the mordant opening of the last movement and the instrumental recitatives which follow, and thereby invests the latter with a peculiar eloquence and firmness. Already at this point one gets the feeling of being present at the finale of all finales. This also fully explains the need for a retrospective examination of the preceding movements, which was subsequently often imitated and which might easily have seemed somewhat artificial. At first, the instruments have the field, then at last, a consummation much to be desired, the theme of joy is heard, played at first, unison, by the basses, in its most primitive form, as it were. It is then developed in several variations until Beethoven, after a preliminary conclusion in the dominant chord—as in a sonata movement—returns to the beginning: a repetition, so to speak, of the first part. It is not until this stage has been reached that everything which the instruments have played so far, i.e., recitatives as well as the theme of joy, the former in an abbreviated form—is repeated, with the addition of the human voice; a *recapitulation* on a higher plane, as it were, an explanation, a glorification of something already there. In this movement, the human voice is nothing more than an additional instrument in the choir of instruments. It is the musical law of *intensification through repetition*— within the limits imposed by the symmetry of the whole— which is applied here on a large scale and which permeates the whole of this music, even in the smallest details.

Just compare with this the childlike, naïve manner in which Liszt seeks to motivate the introduction of the chorus in his *Faust* symphony. Beethoven succeeds in doing exactly the reverse, in making something as apparently illogical as the introduction from without of a recitative and choral movement into a purely orchestral work appear completely natural, convincing and artistically necessary. There is hardly any other example in the history of music which demonstrates so clearly the possibilities of purely abstract music, or offers more convincing proof that it is the musician and the musician alone who is at work therein. Beethoven's virtue lies not in the "idea" as such but in his power to turn this idea so completely into *music*.

A: But how do you explain the fact that people are inclined to read into Beethoven's works not only ideas, but trains of thought alien to music, whole dramatic episodes in fact, to a far greater extent and with far less restraint than in the case of other great composers?

F: This has something to do with a form of self deception which is easily explained. People have always felt that Beethoven achieves a particular kind of definiteness of expression. This exactitude derives from his urge to say whatever he has to say in the shortest and simplest way possible. He is characterised by a particular determination and—a glance at his compositions reveals it—by an extraordinary ability to *simplify*. His surviving notebooks offer abundant evidence of this. We find, for example, that the assurance and simplicity of his thematic construction were not a natural gift, but an achievement. The original form of most of his themes, and frequently of the most beautiful, was more complex than the final form, not, as in the case of other composers, firmly established from the outset, or, as in the case of most modern composers, simpler and more primitive. His creative mind proceeded from chaos to form, towards a conscious simplification, and not, like that of the moderns, into deliberate complexities. It is this characteristic above all which distinguishes Beethoven so clearly from all others, predecessors as well as successors.

There is a further factor which operates in the development, the destiny of these themes, and which I have already referred to as the *logic of spiritual evolution*. The laws of development, of transition from one mood to another, the feeling for what themes, what moods, will blend together to make a new whole, the feeling for the proper sequence of the movements of a work—all represent a kind of spiritual logic which is the essence of the impression Beethoven's music has made on the world. For this logic is *human* in the real and profound meaning of the word. It is at the root of both artistic considerations and human emotions, and it is understood always, at all times. It would of course be rewarding to examine how and why and to what extent spiritual and musical logic coincide in this case; it would be the first step towards answering the far from idle question why a Beethoven symphony is better than so many inferior modern works. The discussion of purely musical forms on the one hand or simple descriptions of the processes of the soul on the other, get us nowhere, for what actually matters is that the spiritual should be perceived in terms of the musical and the latter in terms of the spiritual, that both should be considered *one* and indivisible, so that the very attempt to divide them is a fatal mistake. When prominent musicians disapprove of Beethoven because of the "literary" content of his works, it is to a large extent such misinterpretations which are to blame.

It is the determination to be simple, the musical logic of development which brings about that particular kind of definiteness of expression which strikes the sensitive listener again and again in Beethoven's music. And it is this definiteness which although, as I said before, it is of a purely musical nature, misleads people again and again into looking for more than music and into reading all kinds of things into the score.

A: Have not certain pronouncements made by Beethoven been the source of such misunderstanding?

F: I do not know of a single pronouncement which in itself—without being forcibly interpreted—could give rise to the idea that Beethoven really meant something other by his works than what they are—than as music alone. Wagner's interpretations in this case—however profound Wagner's knowledge of Beethoven in particular may have been otherwise—reveal more about Wagner than about Beethoven. It is in the very nature of music that the clarity of the language it uses is different from the clarity of words: but the language is none the less definite for all that. Choose whichever moment, whichever note you please, in a work by Beethoven you will never have the slightest doubt as to your position within the whole composition. But we are of course dealing with a *musical* whole, which we must be able to hear as such.

Only someone for whom the language of music pure and simple does not suffice would want to interpret Beethoven's exactitude naturalistically in terms of underlying dramas or actual poetry which could be said to have inspired him to composition. Such a person would not know how infinite is the range of music's capacity to express definite meaning to anyone who will only surrender to her language, who can be prevailed upon to speak and understand it. But quite apart from all this, Beethoven has, to put it bluntly, given us neither cause nor right to treat his work in such a manner and to read into it arbitrarily things with which it has nothing whatever to do.

The ideas which his works are meant to embody are a different matter. Thus, Wagner is, to some extent, justified in calling the seventh symphony an "apotheosis of the dance". This has something to do with the curious firmness of Beethoven's musical language mentioned above, with his power of construction, with his particular ability to formulate clearly the essential nature of every work, to render it complete in itself, to *isolate* it. In this sense, almost every one of Beethoven's works represents an idea which could be put into words. But this, as I have said before, is of little importance. Let who will delight in putting these "ideas" into barren words, in impaling the content of something boundlessly alive on the point of an interpretation, like a butterfly on a pin. I personally prefer to stick to the works themselves.

CHAPTER V.

A: I should like to return briefly to the concert we heard the other day. It is surely astonishing how different our Philharmonic Orchestra sounds under different conductors, how it develops different characteristics under each, how it displays under each different virtues and sometimes different vices?

F: There is an element of truth in Bülow's paradox that there is no such thing as a bad orchestra, but only bad conductors. It stands to reason that any orchestra, even the best, is, in the first place, a crowd of different individuals. The extent to which their capabilities and latent potentialities can be made to harmonise, to coalesce, depends on the degree of their integration. But it is this which determines effect. A modest little orchestra which has become an *ensemble* in this sense can be infinitely more impressive than the most accomplished orchestra in existence, if the latter relies on routine.

But unfortunately this is often the case. One could almost say: the better the orchestra, the greater is the temptation for its members—and most of its regular audience too— to be satisfied with mere routine performances, in the utterly mistaken belief that routine is rendered less barren when tempered by technical brilliance.

A: That also, I suppose, explains why the conductor of the last concert asked for so many rehearsals, in spite of the fact that the works performed presented no new problems to the orchestra.

F: The number of rehearsals a conductor needs, provided he has an orchestra of the quality of our Philharmonic, depends on the kind of artist he is, i.e., it depends, partly, on his interpretation of the work—which can differ considerably from one person to another—and partly on his ability to transmit his intentions to the orchestra. There are no absolute rules in this respect. The widely held view that the more rehearsals, the better, is a mistaken one. It would be too easy: after all, the rehearsal as such is not an isolated event. Rehearsal and performance belong together and can be properly understood and appreciated only in interdependence. There are conductors whom years of experience have failed to teach the purpose of rehearsals. But there are others who know how to rehearse interestingly and well and yet are disappointing in public performances. Of course, the rehearsal must fulfil its function as a preparation, i.e., there should be no more improvisation in the actual performance than is absolutely necessary. But there should not be less, either—a point which deserves special emphasis.

A well-known conductor is supposed to have said: one should rehearse until the conductor appears superfluous. This is a fundamental mistake, born of a misconception not only of the arguments for and against having many or few rehearsals but also of the essence and purpose of making music. In the last analysis, a conductor's anxiety to determine everything beforehand down to the smallest detail is caused by his fear of having to rely too much on the inspiration of the moment. By making detailed preparations he attempts to push this inspiration as far as possible into the background, and eventually to replace it entirely and to make it superfluous. He would nail down every single effect, would calculate it as if at his writing desk, would "put it in alcohol". This attitude is wrong because it cannot possibly do justice to *living masterpieces*. The great masterpieces of music are subject to the law of improvisation to a far higher degree than is commonly realised.

There are two reasons why this is so little noticed: one is, that these works are written down. The interpreter gets to know them through the written version. His approach to them is the reverse of their creator's. The latter experiences the real import of what he has to say before or while he commits it to paper; the improvisation on which the written version is based represents the core of the creative process. But as far as the interpreter is concerned, the work is the exact opposite of such improvisation: it is an outer shell of signs and forms which he must pierce if he would penetrate to the work he wishes to perform.

The second reason is that we come to see in these works —especially in the solid masterpieces of the classical period —unalterable and predestined forms which, in their pellu-cidity, seem to be far removed from all seeking, experi-menting and becoming: the exact opposite of "improvisa-tion". Rather they represent a clear and simple system to which the classical composers appear to have adjusted themselves.

In this way we have become the victims of a fallacy implicit in our retroactive point of view. These forms may of course, like the sonata or the fugue, have been previously established. But today we can see clearly with which com-posers, at what time, historically speaking, they began to turn into mere conventions. They did not start as such. They did not exist originally as the fixed conceptions we recognise today. They were discovered gradually, step by step. Yes, it belonged to their very nature that they had to be every time discovered anew and individually. They grew organically, and can only be understood on the basis of their development; they always bear the characteristics of this organic process, wherever they are really alive. Pro-perly understood, they represent a crystallised process of growth, and as such they are the natural precipitate from a process of improvisation. They *are* in fact "improvisation".

This seems to be contradicted by the fact that there are only very few such forms in abstract music, and that these forms (fugue, song, sonata, etc.) are related one to the other or would seem to amount to one and the same for-mula in the end. But is is one of the laws of organic life that a few archetypes embrace infinite possibilities. Musicians who do not understand this may attempt to avoid these archetypes as far as possible; thus Debussy wrote sonatas which were as far removed as possible from sonata form, and Reger composed variations which had very little —if anything—in common with variations in the strict sense of the word.

But we can see how a composer thinks for whom form was itself something living, by taking the case of Beethoven —to stick to the already often quoted and best known example. On a particular occasion, faced with the problem of writing an overture for his one and only opera, Beethoven attempted to throw off the familiar shackles of sonata form. The "Leonora Overture No. II" (the first version of the piece) is a direct description of dramatic events irrespective of sonata form (and disregarding especially the so-called "recapitulation"). A comparison with the "Leonora Overture No. III", the later and final version, is instructive because it throws light not only on the overture itself but also on Beethoven's actual working methods. Wagner thought that this No. III overture surpassed by far in its force of expression everything which followed in the opera *Fidelio*. He considered that its one weakness was the recapitulation, i.e., the point at which the piece stood revealed as an ordinary sonata movement and not as a real direct account of a dramatic event. Wagner therefore sees the weakest point in the passage which Beethoven *had altered*. It is precisely this recapitulation and the somewhat longer coda necessitated by it which distinguish the No. III overture from No. II, and for the sake of which Beethoven re-wrote the piece, a thing he never did in all his life except in this one isolated instance. There are people who still prefer the No. II overture as the "more original version". But it is "more original" only in the sense that it was written earlier. In reality these people fail to realise, just as Wagner did, that the return to sonata form was an innate necessity for Beethoven—that the law of symmetry, of the harmony of the whole, on which the sonata form is based, *compelled him* to do so. It was this and this alone which made possible the climax and the majestic sweep of the coda, the final fulfilment and conclusion of the musical message in the great piece as we know it in the No. III version. As far as Beethoven was concerned, in this as in all his other works, the sonata form was not something to be adopted or disregarded at will. It was conceived and grew naturally as part of every work. It was the inevitable consequence of such a conception; it was *the* form of Beethoven's musical thought, because it was an essentially natural form. Whoever examines the two overtures without prejudice will agree that the later version was justified, however much he may admire the genius which went to the making of the earlier. Beethoven knew what he was doing when he rewrote the piece.

But we do not know. On the whole we are quite ignorant of the meaning of "form". Right through the whole musical life of today a cleavage is distinguishable between those who still have an inkling, a remembrance of this knowledge, and those who have already lost it. This knowledge springs only from nature—but "Form is a secret to most", as Goethe says.

When men have lost the feeling for real form, when they have forgotten that its origin is improvisation, they begin to search for substitutes, for supports and buttresses to save the tottering edifice. The "literary" programme seemed for a while to offer such support. Later, composers avoided writing abstract music altogether and wrote only for the theatre. They took refuge in the drama, and finally restricted themselves to choreographic representations. The less capable people became of writing in accordance with the laws of music, of expressing their thoughts in organically developed forms, the greater was their need for variety introduced from without. The result is that antithesis is no longer desired—and this is a fundamental difference—in order to form a new synthesis, but contrasts are sought for their own sake. A piece of music is no longer, as it used to be, an organism developed in accordance with the law of its own being, with a centre of gravity of its own; but is becoming, to an ever increasing extent, a means of entertainment, lacking a centre of gravity, designed merely to offer a modicum of variety. This means that entirely different criteria have to be applied and entirely different aspects considered. The same considerations belong equally to the performance of music—for, as I have already said, interpretation in any age follows the same direction as creation, and it is the great creative forces that decisively influence an epoch. Thus it could not fail to happen that the growing demands of our own age for variety and entertainment should also begin to make themselves felt in the performance of works that were originally conceived quite differently.

The law of improvisation, which we have described as the condition precedent for the evolution of all true form, demands that the artist should identify himself completely with a work and its growth. If the power to shape, the omnipresent feeling for genuine form are relaxed, all this is immediately changed; the performer is no longer absorbed by the work, he consciously detaches himself from it, only momentarily at first, but always more and more. He no longer experiences the work directly, but becomes increasingly a controller, an observer, an arranger. Forces are released which had heretofore been bound together by the compulsion of living the work. One has time "to spare" for all kinds of things outside, behind and beyond the work. A young colleague of mine once asked me what I did with my left hand while conducting. While I was pondering my reply I suddenly realised that I had never asked myself that particular question before, although I had been a conductor for more than twenty years. One starts thinking about oneself only when all one's powers are no longer engaged in attention to and concentration upon the work. It is then that one learns to "pose", an expedient used particularly by conductors, and something for which a real artist should have simply no time. One also begins to pay special attention to technical mastery: technique begins unnoticed to become an end in itself. But this means that one loses the power of recognising that the soul must be form and form, soul; one loses nothing less than the instinctive feeling for the cogency and truth of artistic development.

A: I am quite sure that modern audiences are not at all aware of this. Surely there must be other symptoms?

F: Of course there are, and our audiences would react to them in an entirely different manner had they not largely lost their instinct. The lack of inward veracity becomes most apparent in passages where spiritual expression comes into the open. Thus it is possible to tell from the treatment of the so-called *rubato* for instance—which is a temporary relaxation of rhythm under the stress of emotion—as from a barometer reading, whether or not the impulses provoking it are in accordance with the real feeling of the passage or not, whether they are genuine or not. For as soon as this *rubato* is "put on" and is intentional and calculated, it becomes, as it were, automatically exaggerated. This is less noticeable with an orchestra, where it is technically difficult to achieve owing to the number of instruments involved, although a false *rubato* can frequently be heard even there. But amongst pianists, to whom these restrictions do not apply, there is a tendency nowadays to use this trick un-restrainedly, with positively devastating results. In such cases, where the artist has the work "in his hands", where he can do with it what he will, that inward mendacity which is the real cause of false *rubato* can bring about all its disastrous consequences. Thus pianists—taking them by and large—render themselves ineffective although they have for their own the most beautiful music ever composed for any instrument. But the public merely shuts both eyes and does not appear to notice anything.

But there are other tricks apart from the *rubato* which are designed to enable the performer to simulate what he cannot feel. We have already mentioned the conductor's pose. A lack of discrimination between those movements of a conductor's which are helpful and necessary and those which are wrong, affected, put on, "posed", is a distinguishing feature of metropolitan audiences. It would almost seem as though the latter considered poses as absolutely indispensable, as though the performance of a conductor or of a pianist lacked spice without them. People have become incapable of distinguishing between an expressive gesture inspired by the work and addressed to the orchestra and an empty gesture designed to impress the audience.

At first sight it would seem to be an advantage that energies are thus liberated which can be applied to problems of technical control. But this is a mistake. As I have said before, the moment that technical problems are treated as ends in themselves, the spiritual unity of the whole is destroyed. In a good performance the technical aspect should not be divorced even for seconds from the "spiritual" aspect, not even when it would be "effective" in itself. Granted, it may produce an effect, but it is nevertheless an illegitimate effect since it detracts from what is essential. But of course, the only people who can feel and know this are those who are already familiar with the work from a previous performance commensurate with its true nature. This is the reason why such interpretations of the great living masterpieces of the past, based on technical virtuosity, are so dangerous in practice: they thoroughly corrupt taste. The kind of performance designed to display virtuosity, effect and variety, all of them put on from outside, is bound to stimulate and develop corresponding characteristics in the audience. Thus the whole of music making loses to an ever-increasing extent the weight and the measure of inward necessity which hitherto—and here I speak as a German about Germany—it has always possessed.

Everything connected purely with problems of technique and virtuosity is largely a matter of training. And thus we see that, even in the case of the performer, a tendency to practise excessively and to determine every little detail in advance is not only readily combined with a performance designed to produce an effect of virtuosity and variety, but that the latter is actually demanded by the former. After all, one cannot "practise" anything except details; but the effects of the virtuoso are effects of detail, effects of variety, of contrast, quite apart from an "organic" whole. One cannot "finish", calculate, "put in alcohol" anything but details; a unity complete in itself, on the other hand, always remains to some extent incommensurable. But no one who considers this quality of incommensurability to be the final essential element will ever overestimate the importance of practising, with all due deference to the need for it. Thus we see that the performer's mentality is revealed even in his methods of training.

A: If the rehearsal ought only to be a preparation which has nothing to do with that final, essential element, is it then possible for the conductor, on the night, to convey this element the "incommensurable", as you call it, to his orchestra?

F: This is a subject on which one could write volumes. But it is a fact that the point at which this element of spiritual incommensurability and the technical exigencies and achievements of our time meet is still, even in our present state of knowledge, the real *terra incognita*. If you ask whether, to what extent, and why a conductor can impart this "essential element" to the orchestra, you will, at best, be told that it is a question of "personality", of

"suggestion" or the like. It is anything but that, of course—
if the concept of personality is taken to denote something
mystically indefinable. It is much more a question of real
things, things for which there are names and which are
mysterious only in so far as they are connected without
exception with the spiritual aspect of an artist's work.
Anybody who thinks today that it is possible to impart and
develop the "technique" of a singer, instrumental player
or conductor in the absence of close and constant association with the art itself, in the face of which technique can
only be a means, is very much mistaken. Problems of "technique" are exerting a hypnotic influence on us nowadays,
and considerable progress has been made in the examination of its foundations—especially by means of the modern
biological approach. No matter whether it is a question of
ski-ing or of playing the piano—we are in a position today
to achieve considerably better results in a considerably
shorter period of time than we were a few decades ago. The
trouble is that, unlike skiers, artists have become not better
but worse as far as the decisive point, i.e., the capacity for
direct artistic expression is concerned, in the process. It is
difficult to influence a technique acquired as an end in
itself, but such a technique nevertheless radiates its own
influence: standardised technique creates in return standardised art. We have not even begun to realise to what
extent this process—which can be observed all over
Europe—has made inroads in Germany. It moves too
slowly for us to have become aware of it; we have grown
too much accustomed to it. The result of it all is that art is
being deprived more and more of its essence and of its soul,
which, to everybody's surprise, seems increasingly superfluous the greater its technical perfection. And this applies
to creation as much as to interpretation.

Do not misunderstand me: I am not opposed to highly
developed technique as such. I, too, would not want to be
without its benefits. What I dislike and what worries me

profoundly is the chasm which has opened up between our knowledge of the technical and that of the "spiritual" aspect of music. In the former we may be titans and heroes, but in the latter we are surely nowadays nothing more than children.

CHAPTER VI.

A: I saw you last night at the concert given by the French conductor X. Can an international exchange of artists ever be fruitful in the deeper sense in an art like music, which would on the face of it seem to have strongly national characteristics?

F: Such an exchange is absolutely necessary for us, both as musicians and as men. Ever since Europe and European music have existed, there has been this exchange, whether the powers that be were for or against it. Politics and the life of art are not one and the same thing.

A: It is nevertheless claimed in the political sphere today that art must adapt itself to politics and must serve them. At any rate it cannot be denied that to a certain extent art is subject to national limitations. This is proved in a way by these exchange concerts.

F: All art bears witness to the innermost reality of a nation, and music in particular to a much greater extent than any other art, is admittedly subject in some way to national limitations. But surely not in the way in which the politicians imagine it to be. Art is not concerned with markets, doctrines, communism, democracy and the like. Nor has art got anything to do with the nationalism of power politics and conquest. It has no truck with hatred between nations wherever, however, or from whatever reason this may arise. It testifies not to the politics of a nation—ephemeral as they are in the nature of things—but rather to its eternal essence. Art does not express a nation's hate, but its love. It portrays man when he is "himself", harmless, trusting, simple, proud, a member of a happy, all-embracing humanity. No matter how different the nations of Europe may be—as different as only individualities can be—they are connected by a common, invisible, subterranean bond. In this sense we can go so far as to claim that music, more than any other art the "last" European art, has an eminently political function. Music, which seems to be the least real of all the arts, appears to offer, more than any other art, the final proof that "Europe" is not a purely fantastic conception, the figment of an idle brain. Nowhere will the German meet the Italian with less reserve, nowhere will he understand him better, than in the masterpieces of Raphael, Titian or Verdi. Nowhere does the Russian appear more rational and lovable than in his great writers and composers. And where does the enigmatical German understand himself better, where is he better understood and even loved by other nations than in Bach and Beethoven, Schubert and Mozart?

A: Nevertheless it can hardly be denied that the division into nations as it has developed in the course of time is making itself felt more and more in the sphere of music. German and French music are today wide apart both in form and sentiment.

F: Exactly, as it must with individualities. There are severances, there is conflict, tension between them, but there is also much which they have in common, spheres in which the other is felt to be not a contrast, but a complement. This is proved in particular by the history of European music. Have not Wagner, Verdi, and Bizet equally conquered the "world"? To keep to Germany, did not purely German composers like Bach and Beethoven, and more recently in a certain sense even Brahms, become part of the totality of European experience?

Of course, every nation, just like every individual, has a tendency to be self-sufficient, to isolate itself, and to stress its own achievements. And if people once thought and hoped that modern means of communication and modern methods of establishing points of contact or mutual understanding would bring about the end of nationalist segregation and chauvinism, they have been mistaken. In many cases the existence of numerous points of contact between the nations would seem to have brought about the exact opposite of mutual understanding, i.e., fear of foreign influence, leading to excessive self-importance in individual nations. Such self-importance—on whatever it may be based—is not what it pretends to be, namely, a sign of strength. Would it not have been better if Debussy had refrained from deliberately writing in the margin of his violin sonatas "musicien Français"? And we cannot agree with those who could celebrate Bruckner as a particularly "German" composer because to this day it is in Germany that he is most appreciated. We have no intention of decrying the Frenchman's liking for Debussy, or the German's predilection for Bruckner. But even if it were true that Debussy can be entirely appreciated only by a Frenchman, and Bruckner by a German, that would not make either of them better. It would be more to the point to concentrate on those aspects of their work in which they are not merely expressing limited, national characteristics, but which belong to the totality of European musicians.

A: In view of the present isolation and segregation of nations I am bound to ask: what is it that causes such a definite separation between these individuals—for it is as such that we must consider the nations? Is it more difficult today for them to find the way to each other than it was in the past. For thousands of years Europe was a cultural entity. Is it no longer such an entity today?

F: Let us first consider the past. In bygone ages the Christian religion represented a common soil. Since it was thrust aside, there has remained only the nation—for the composer *needs* a native soil. Thus, since the eighteenth century, in music nationality has increasingly taken the place of religion, although admittedly without ousting it completely until the present day. The strength that is still left in religion is demonstrated by the fact that really great composers whose life's work was concerned with an entirely different sphere, like Brahms and Verdi, showed their vitality as late as the nineteenth century by their ability to write genuine and living church music without sacrificing the special character of their other works. They are of course exceptions; on the whole musical progress in the course of the past two centuries has been rooted in the soil of the individual nations. Even the supra-national art of Bach, Beethoven, Wagner, etc., was born of and conditioned by the nation: it is German. With Berlioz, Schubert, Chopin, Smetana, Tchaikovsky, Grieg, Verdi and Brahms the broad flow of European music divided into various single streams in the course of the nineteenth century. All of these artists were conscious of a common origin. They remained Europeans no matter how strongly they also represented their own nations. Through them the various nations made their contribution to the history of music, one after another, and Europe discovered herself anew in her music. Only much later, only with the beginning of the twentieth century, only with Reger, Debussy and so on did the development of individual national characteristics progress so far that mutual understanding began to get more difficult. It was then that men began to search more and more for a type of music which would eliminate this dependence on the individual nations. People thought that they could find such music by appealing not to the nation, but to the "epoch". Composers no longer turned to the ordinary man with all his national limitations but rather to "modern" man as such, and believed that in so doing they were initiating a new era of liberty.

Time enough has now gone by to give us a certain perspective in this regard too. History would seem to teach us that every type of artistic expression requires certain limitations to enable it to find itself. The "new" music claims above all to be contemporary. It replaces allegiance to a nation with a rather more fleeting and more questionable allegiance to an epoch.

A: However that may be, is not all the talk of "new", "contemporary" music, clear and simple as it is when contrasted with the multiplicity of nations, bound to exert considerable influence on European music?

F: Undoubtedly, within a certain area. But looking at it as a whole one has to admit that European music has never presented such a picture of mutually exlusive endeavours as it does today, whose protagonists are ready to fight each other to the death. What formerly seemed abundance is now sheer chaos. Once upon a time, when the souls of nations first flowed into music, men were tolerant. The doors stood wide open. France received Schumann, and, at a later date, Russian music; Russia received Beethoven and Brahms, Italy German music, and Germany Italian, French and Russian music—a picture of general growth and development, without prejudice to a common fund of common tradition. It was in the dispute between the followers of Wagner and those of Brahms in Vienna, in the argument over the "Zukunftsmusik" of Wagner and Liszt in Germany (in which Berlioz too became involved in France) that an apparently irreconcilable opposition was revealed for the first time which prompted each party to consider the other as its deadly enemy—the opposition between "conservative" music and the "new" music, which eventually developed into a consistent system of atonality. We are not dealing here with an antithesis within the traditional meaning of the word—all mere "antitheses" can after all be reduced to a common denominator—but with contrasts which simply admit of no synthesis, with a life and death struggle in which no holds are barred. Contrasts between national characteristics which had existed all along were now emphasised anew and exploited with a sharpness that was previously lacking. The feeling of a common loyalty to a higher authority ceased to exist. The state, the powers that be, have taken the helm in musical matters since Music herself seems incapable of steering her own course. Can we really say that the differences of nature, ability, and will within European man—always of course including America in this context—have imperceptibly become so great that we can no longer speak of a common European civilisation? Is this the end of Europe?

Next comes the question: Who is turning the whole of artistic and intellectual Europe into an armed camp? Where are the exponents of these contrasts? In trying to get clear about this it strikes us that it is not so much the works or the personalities of the leading artists which appear so hostile and irreconcilable one with the other, but rather what one might call the "atmosphere" enveloping them. The men themselves are much closer to each other than they think; the more so since, being contemporaries or members of the same nation, they are faced with the same or similar tasks. It is the "atmosphere" surrounding them as manifested in style, in a common vehicle of artistic expression, which varies from school to school, tendency to tendency, and artist to artist. I would call this atmosphere, this common language of the artist, his idiom. "Idiom" in my interpretation of the word does not denote what an artist says, but rather his medium and the manner in which he says it. It is this aspect of a work of art which has a decisive influence on the first impression it makes, which first meets the eye, but which is not by any means identical with the work of art itself. Whenever it is highly developed, it tends to conceal rather than reveal the real message of an individual work. It is the idiom of their music rather than its real content which stamps, let us say, Mozart as the laughing rococo cavalier, and Wagner—who is to apt to be misunderstood—as a sensual, melodramatic and hyper-romantic creature in the eyes of the superficial observer.

Idiom is extremely significant so long as art is examined as the style and the language of a period. But it ceases to be significant when we are dealing with the essence of art as revealed in individual works of art alone. Had Mozart really been nothing more than an incarnation of the tendencies and conventions of the rococo period, he would long since have ceased to matter to us. With Wagner, of course, the effect of his "idiom", that combination peculiar to him of harmony, orchestral sound, leitmotiv technique, endless melody and mannerisms of all kinds, both on the stage and in the orchestra pit was so powerful and, on its first impact, so stunning, that even a man like Verdi lost his creative powers for a while under its influence. At that time everyone attempted to imitate Wagner's style; a whole generation of Wagnerians grew up. It was not until later that experience showed this to be impossible, and the strength of his music was seen to lie not in its idiom, its style, and its scintillating surface, but in something quite different.

Now the idiom changes not only from generation to generation, but from work to work. This is particularly noticeable in Wagner's works. The idiom, i.e., the spiritual climate and the musical texture, of, for example, *Tristan und Isolde* is quite different from that of *Die Meistersinger von Nürnberg* or *Parsifal*. But experience has shown time and again that the disciples, followers and worshippers of such work are simply incapable of distinguishing between the work itself and its idiom. They are completely at the mercy of the influence of the idiom. This is shown again and again, especially by the imitations of such works and styles. Only detached observers or people of a later generation are in a position to judge how very far such imitations fall short of the "original". Those who are completely enveloped in one idiom are simply incapable of conducting a fruitful argument with anybody else, unless it is someone who owes allegiance to the same "idiom". Once this stage has been reached, there is nothing left but instinctive egocentricity, uncompromising self-adulation, obtuse animosity and hostility towards everything different. We experience it every day; a man who believes in Strawinsky's

methods will find it extremely difficult to admit that it is
possible to say things worth saying in the idiom of Wagner
or Strauss, and it is rare indeed to find a man accustomed
to thinking in terms of Bruckner's or Reger's music who
can be just to Debussy or Strawinsky.

It is a different matter as far as the creator, the originator
of the idiom is concerned. Since it signifies to him only a
means of expression and in no sense the work itself, he
would seem to be less subject to its influence than anybody
else. Thus the impression made all over the world by
Goethe's *Werther* was essentially due to its idiom; it was
really a period-piece to which everybody succumbed at the
time with the exception of the man who had created it and
was therefore proof against its fascination: Goethe himself.
A similar case occurred later in Wagner's *Tristan*, the
"idiom" and style of which appear to be particularly highly
developed amongst Wagner's works. What a lot of harm
this "Tristan" style has wrought in music! And here again,
the only person who did not succumb to it was its creator.
Immediately after he had finished *Tristan* he started work
on *Die Meistersinger*, which represents the greatest imaginable contrast with *Tristan*, not only in its message, but
especially also in its idiom.

It is particularly with Wagner's works in mind that we
can say that just as the effect of his idiom contributed once
upon a time to his world-wide success, so this idiom, now
that the first fascination has worn off and the phenomenon
of Wagner is beginning to be historic, has come to bar the
way to the genuine effect of his art. If in his own lifetime it
was inclined to veil, or even to make unrecognisable with
its obtrusive brilliance, Wagner's genuinely creative characteristics, today it intervenes wholly between him and his
hearers. It is entirely due to this idiom if in his native land,
of all places, this composer has become the most misunderstood of the great ones. Is not the whole of the voluminous
literature which has been directed against Wagner—start-

ing from Nietzsche by way of the followers of Brahms right down to Strawinsky—directed almost exclusively against Wagner's idiom, which is tacitly and wrongly identified with his actual works?

It is these different "idioms" which, as in the case of Wagner, sow discord amongst Europeans today. Every one of them pretends to represent not only reality, or an atmosphere, but also a programme, a postulate, a system of orthodoxy, if not a science. A whole army of "experts"— we are living in the age of experts—is engaged in giving a foundation of theory to the various idioms, in demonstrating their efficacy as the sole purveyors of celestial bliss and in pitting one against the next. But there are limits to this process. In contrast to the work of art itself, the idiom is bound to lose its effect in the course of time. It fades, it becomes "historical". But as its effect disappears so do the contrasts of which it was once the incarnation. Today, half a century later, we find that Wagner and Brahms do not seem to us to differ from each other as much as they themselves thought they did. The various "idioms" can be reduced to a common denominator just like individuals or nations if only the view point chosen be sufficiently distant. Thus we can see distinctly even today that many of the storms which until recently ravaged the surface of European music are now subsiding.

There would seem to remain only one insuperable contrast: the contrast which first appeared in neo-German "Zukunftsmusik" and which has since developed into atonal music with its doctrine of exclusiveness. This contrast can be described with some justification as a "political" one. We shall discuss it and its causes elsewhere.

A: Surely the fight against individualism proves that modern man is painfully aware of this complete lack of common fundamental ideas and concepts in present-day Europe. The younger generation in particular sees the real enemy in this very "individualism".

F: Quite so; the history of music was revised with this point in view in the years immediately after the first world war. Whereas the nineteenth century, and even the age of Wagner and Brahms, had seen in Beethoven the crowning glory of the history of music, succeeding generations quite unmistakably turned to Bach and more or less decried Beethoven. A system of Bruckner orthodoxy was evolved in Germany under this motto, and a school of composers was eventually brought into being which found its exemplars exclusively in the pre-Bach and pre-Handel eras, when, it was thought, the need for the great "I am" and with it odious "individualism" had not yet arisen. This would be all very well, if only our position today were not entirely different from that of the pre-Bach era. For then, when everyone really lived and moved and had his being in natural harmony with his time and age, people were not at all conscious of the fact. And what people were conscious of and deliberately aimed at might easily have sounded to modern ears like the purest "individualism". It is certainly not the consciousness of the need for an artistic crisis which brings one about, for it is impossible, and merely love's labour lost, to try to bring back to life a situation belonging to the past, no matter how recent that past may be, by conscious means, i.e., by mere *perception*, however profound and comprehensive. No matter how desirable such a situation may appear to us at the moment, the very fact that we have become aware of its desirability, of the need for it, renders its return impossible. *Innocence once lost can never be regained by conscious means; for really creative powers are operative only in the state of innocence.*

Generally speaking, it should be pointed out that the relationship between the individual and society, on which the existence of the artist finally depends, is completely proof against the influence of the conscious will. The form this relationship takes in individual cases is ordained by fate and must be accepted like one's station in life, one's nation

and one's race. But it is this, and not desires based on *perception*, which decides whether or not a man *shall be numbered amongst the creative artists.*

A: You spoke of artists who lived and worked in opposition to their times. Are they not predominantly those whose art was misunderstood by their contemporaries, who did not have enough "success"—as popularly understood—in their capacity as artists?

F: What I referred to does not depend on outward success. An artist's innermost feeling for life (and we are at the moment discussing artists only) remains the same, no matter whether his works are successes or failures. Thus we find in the ranks of those whose lives and work were opposed to their environment men like Michelangelo, Wagner, etc., who attained a vast measure of outward success. The matter goes deeper. If there had been no powerful laws of convention demanding universal allegiance the great Greek tragedies could never have been written, based as they were on the revolt of the individual against eternal laws and on his destruction as the most profound and valid *acknowledgment*, as it were, of these laws. It is the personal tragedy of many great artists that they experience these eternal laws, that is to say, the foundations of our communal life, more deeply than society itself which on the whole is fully unaware of them. The "titanism" of a Beethoven or a Michelangelo is profoundly moving, not because it is the expression of "unfettered individualism"— generally speaking genuine individualism is completely at a loss when faced with such artistic phenomena—but for the very opposite reason: the fate of such artists is moulded by their experience of a *law* which they cannot escape but to which they are subject and which they must accept. And it is this fate which will be found to operate in their life and work.

A: Human nature is such that contemporaries as well as succeeding generations will persist in mistakenly attempting to interpret this fate in a strictly personal sense, as the product—psychologically speaking—of successes, and even more, of failures. There is, however, one question which forces itself upon our attention: why is it that great artists, who are usually inclined to take the subjects of their tragedies from real life, seem to fight shy of giving artistic expression to the one tragedy which concerns them directly: the tragedy of the artist as such? As far as I know there are hardly any descriptions of the fate of the artist on this earth to be found among the works of the great artists.

F: I do not think I know of a single attempt in this direction made by a real artist, with the exception of Pfitzner's *Palestrina*. In the works of so all embracing a writer as Goethe, for example, "the artist" hardly ever comes to the fore, at any rate not in the sense in which Goethe himself lived an artist's life. It is rather the bourgeois romanticists, the limited but sentimental minds, who have a preference for the lives of artists. The artist's own eyes are on his work. He says to himself, "what if it is a tragedy to be an artist (one could also say, a genius)? There is no point in dwelling upon it, which might at the most make me unfit to bear it; and borne it *must* be". The artist is therefore much more likely to fight against his environment, from which he must wrest every demand, every work. This has nothing whatever to do with "success" or "failure". It was at the height of his triumph that Wagner in his later pamphlets fulminated in bitterness and desperation against a world from which naturally-talented "creative" man, i.e., he himself, his life, his struggle, was to be *methodically and deliberately eliminated*.

But this brings us to something different: Wagner's struggle in this respect was the struggle of a modern artist against a modern environment, i.e., an attempt at a showdown between the artist and the present-day world. But the latter has at its disposal far more formidable weapons than it had in the past. Whereas the past countered as it were with lance and sword, the present works with poison gas. Perhaps in an earlier age it was precision of expression which guaranteed the artist's effect. What mattered in the last analysis was the receptivity of the audience, the standards of criticism and taste: i.e., an instinctive, more or less sub-conscious factor. The struggle between the artist and his environment could only end in the artist's victory, provided that he really was an artist, provided, that is, that he had something to say and was capable of saying it clearly and validly. But today another factor enters the field, a kind of auto-suggestion which, coming from the conscious mind, deprives natural criticism and taste of every element of clearness and certainty: namely, historical knowledge. It has gradually become one of the functions of the history of art and of the contemplation of art, to attempt *to explain us to ourselves*. It is no longer the business of the artists in our midst to teach us who we are, nor do we find ourselves reflected in them, as bygone productive ages did, but the *expert historian* tells the artist what manner of man he should be, and dictates to him on the strength of his knowledge how he should feel, think and create. The consequences of this development are incalculable. We are living in the age of science—the history of art is a science—and we believe in science alone and not in super-rational things such as—expressed in terms of the subject under discussion —feeling and taste. Thus, in accordance with a kind of knowledge abstracted from the work of his immediate predecessors, the artist is denied all sovereignty, liberty, directness of expression: He is told what he must do and what he must not do, what he must feel and what he must endeavour to attain in order to strike an answering chord, in order to be "modern".

A man trained in the discipline of history invariably makes his claims upon the modern artist on the grounds of historical analogy. But since historical situations never literally repeat themselves, analogies are invariably false, no matter how compelling they may appear at first sight. What is really "modern" assumes a different form from that postulated by theory, since historical perception and the creation of something "new" out of the subconscious present are diametrically opposed to each other, and *the one can never take the place of the other*. The adage that "a politician can at best only learn from history how not to do things and never how to do them" applies even more to the artist. An insight into the historical necessities of all ages is of no assistance at all to the artist in composing new works or in understanding his own times.

But there is another reason why in Germany today so very much importance is attached to historical perception of all kinds. As a perfunctory glance at modern publications on music will show, it is used only too often to bolster up defective and uncertain feeling. Some time ago I attended a performance of the *St. Matthew Passion*. Apart from some good performances by the soloists, this—one of the most soul stirring masterpieces in the history of music—made an impression of unparalleled aridity and tedium. Imagine, therefore, my surprise when I read in the papers on the following day that at long last an exemplary performance of the *St. Matthew Passion* had been given. According to the present state of knowledge the old instruments used and the small choir were similar to those used by Bach. The small choir in particular had made it possible to reproduce for the first time the full impression of Bach's polyphony. The music critic had apparently failed to notice that all "polyphony" had simply been thrown to the winds in the performance in question. As if polyphony were a problem of numbers and not of interpretation, as if one could not be just as "polyphonous", given enough space, with a choir of 500 as with one of 50 members, as if an orchestra could not be as polyphonous as a string quartet. The orchestra admittedly played accurately and the singers sang correctly, but we did not hear a single phrase which had really taken shape, not a single melody inspired from within, not a single polyphonic line which was really felt. The music of Bach did not as it were put in an appearance at all. But it was apparently this which our "historically" trained music critic thought was most in keeping with Bach's idea "in accordance with the present state of knowledge".

When a person recites a poem or gives a lecture he endeavours in the first instance to enunciate the words in such a manner that their *sense* is intelligible. If we listened attentively, we should notice that this is accomplished by means of almost imperceptible, almost imponderable little stresses—a slight hesitation here, intensification there, now a stress, then a drop. Yet it is this and this alone which enables the listener to understand what he is hearing, especially when the sentences are long and complicated. The only condition precedent is that the reciter or lecturer should himself know what he is saying, i.e., that he should understand the meaning of what he recites. This sounds like a commonplace but it is anything but a commonplace, as far as musicians are concerned. The spoken word sounds right only if the speaker himself understands what he is saying; music, when it is sung or played, acquires the right tone, the right form, which makes it intelligible to the audience only if the performer has himself experienced it. Now it was this tone and form which were lacking in the performance described above; the work had not been understood and was therefore unintelligible for all is impeccability. Admittedly nothing was "romanticised" or "sentimentalised"—as if the natural rendering of a natural phrase were tantamount to romanticising or sentimentalising, i.e., in plain English to *falsifying*. The very fact that in this performance Bach had nothing, absolutely nothing, to say to the famished heart seemed to inspire our music critic with inordinate satisfaction. Did he not know that fear of sentimentality is nothing but fear of something in one's own heart? That whoever fights shy of sentimentality—i.e. of superficial, spurious, exaggerated and affected sensibility instead of genuine feeling—thereby reveals that he must *fear* it, in that he lacks or at any rate is deficient in natural sentiment? Sentimentality is alien to a man in full possession of his spiritual power. There is no need for him to be afraid of it, nor does he avoid moments of genuine absorption. Nobody can convince me that Bach's congregation sang the chorale, "When I must leave this vale of tears", with the same emotions and therefore with the same expression as, let us say, "God guideth all things for the best". Why then should *we* sing it like that? Because we are afraid of our own feelings?

When looked at with a modicum of detachment—which is how we must look at it—the whole thing is the wildest farce imaginable. The fear of sentimentality, *the fear of oneself* as the motto of the music of a whole generation! Music should be a glorious affirmation of self, if it is to have *any sense at all*.

But this is only one aspect. Because people feel, in the uncomfortable, demanding society of classical music as if they were wearing corsets, they let themselves go when they are dealing with contemporary works where they think they are on safer ground. Especially when works of the so-called "late romantic period" are given, those very people whose performance had been imbued with the cold spirit of objectivity all at once indulge in spurious emotion, in false, calculated *rubato*, etc. All of a sudden we realise of course why they fought shy of sentiment: they had every reason for doing so. They are opposed to individualism because they are afraid of the licentious "individual" within themselves.

A: Is that really the whole reason? Or has our attitude towards the individual and his claims changed compared with that of an earlier age, even the nineteenth century?

F: Of course it has changed, and I should be the last to

deny the existence of those almost imperceptible yet definite changes in the attitude of whole epochs, of that change
of perspective, unnoticed yet on the whole pronounced and
weighty, which we call historic development. Whether we
like it or not we are all in the midst of this "development",
day by day. And every attempt, even the smallest, really to
escape from it or to oppose it from within is immediately
punished by Nature with the only sentence she can pro-
nounce, the most dreadful punishment of all—sterility.

There can be no doubt that today we are incapable of
taking a naïve delight in the expression of untrammelled
personality as people did for example in the early Renaissance period, the period of "classical" music, the romantic
era, etc. In those ages humanity rediscovered as it were, after
long spells of collective inertia, the fascination of the
"individual". Today we have become allergic to the mere
individual, to all kinds of ivory towers, to all arbitrary and
premature limitations in favour of the individual. We have
become conscious to a much higher degree of our limitations and our dependence on society, on our nation and
our age. But because we have learned this lesson—largely
by the discipline of historical analysis which we have
passed—we can and must try to see the other side. For we
are not mere dayflies, helpless under the passage of time:
we are also eternal, indestructible beings, made in the
image of God—not only products of a certain generation,
members of a particular class and group, but also definite,
unique, incomparable individual souls answerable only to
ourselves. Translated into terms of art, this means that
every work of art has two aspects, one turned towards its
own "time" and one towards eternity. Just as we can say
that man is different, new, at every moment, that it is the
task of the artist to record his mutability, dependence and
limitations, so we can say that the human soul has been
the same since time immemorial, that the artist must record
its eternal essence, its unique quality and indestructibility.

And here we are approaching again but from a different direction the contrast between the art historian and the artist. The subject of the historian is the development of art in the course of history, whereas that of the artist is the isolated incident. Individuals matter to the historian only in so far as they are comparable; to the artist only in so far as they are incomparable. The historian adopts an attitude of superiority, distracts our attention from ourselves, leads us to contemplation and knowledge. He aims in the last analysis at mastery over the multiplicity of phenomena. But the artist brings us—every one of us—face to face with his creation, forces us to wrestle with him just as he is wrestling with us; it is surrender he wants, not mastery. Where the historian is the man of discriminating intelligence, the artist is the man of—love.

CHAPTER VII

The first six conversations recorded in this volume were conducted in 1937. We are now in the year 1947. To tackle directly the questions with which I intend to deal requires a certain amount of intelligent spontaneity. I am fully aware of the fact that I shall gratify neither myself nor others by grasping this red hot poker. The musicians of today usually take one side or the other. The technique of atonality is more than a method of musical expression. For many it is a working hypothesis without which they could not compose music at all. But thus it becomes a matter of life and death, so that one might well feel disinclined to discuss the arguments for and against it *sine ira et studio*.

Yet it is this which is needed. As a matter of fact nothing is needed more, if we are to have any hopes of winning free of the present turmoil and distress to a happier future.

I consider myself qualified to say a word in this connection mainly because of my experiences as a conductor. I have now been active in a position of responsibility for more than 30 years. During the whole of this period—the period in which "modern music" first came into vogue in Germany—there were few important concert works by prominent composers which did not pass through my hands. I have unreservedly devoted time, concentration, and energy even to those works to which my personal inclination did not attract me. It need not surprise anyone that there were works of importance which were not quite to my liking. It is not the task of the conductor, or of any interpretive artist—as many people who subscribe to mistaken ideas as to the nature of musical performances imagine—to report as "objectively" as possible, to "lecture" as it were on the piece of music to be performed, but to bring this music go glowing life with as much passion and affection as he is capable of. And if the artist must

proceed *sine ira et studio* in the *choice* of the works to be produced, passionate partisanship must be his aim in their *performance*. Thus I openly confess that as a musician— not to mention as a composer—I am a convinced partisan of tonality, although it cannot be denied that the latter has undergone remarkable expansion in the last few years. To refrain from using the resources which it offers to every musician who really knows how to handle it, and to wish nostalgically for a return to the state of affairs before the discovery of the laws of tonality, or for the limitation of those laws and resources, would seem to me like wishing to return to the days of the post-chaise, when we have wireless and motor-cars at our disposal. In spite of all this, atonality claims to have progressed beyond tonality; it claims to represent an expansion, and an emancipation from the narrow world of tonal relationships. There can indeed be no doubt that the claim is justified to a certain extent, and that atonality must be considered as an expression of these puzzling times. To attempt to determine what part it actually plays is one of the principal tasks of the present day.

I hear from London that following the war there has been a manysided and to all appearances vital interest in concert life there. Unfortunately the distaste of the public for so-called "modern" music is making itself felt more and more. Tchaikovsky and Beethoven are more than ever the box-office attractions. Put a piece of Debussy on the programme (not to mention a really modern work) and the box-office receipts are bound to drop. Private performances of works by contemporary composers are extremely badly attended.

The informant who told me of this is full of indignation about such a state of affairs. The public, he says, is more than ever interested in easy pleasure. It has in no sense measured up to the task of evaluating, following and stimulating the development of contemporary music. It is, he says, just as irresponsible and lazy as always. All those who are genuinely interested in the future of music are filled with sorrow at what is happening.

Let us put it quite clearly: no-one understands this development, no-one knows how to take it. And yet it would be better if, instead of disapproving of these things, or pretending they do not exist, we asked ourselves how matters can have come to such a pass, and what can be the real reason for this attitude on the part of audiences. It would be better if instead of subjecting the so-called "public" to moral censure—a thankless task at the best of times—we realised that we are here faced with a problem. So far this has not been generally realised, at least not by those who care for the future of music. It is only by recognising the problem as such, and by facing it, that we can hope to find a solution.

It is an old truth that people prefer to hear things which they know already. The reason is certainly not to be found in their indolence alone, but also in a desire to rediscover, to surrender themselves again and again to a work they love and trust. Musicians have always worried their heads over the question of why certain works stand so much to the fore and are always being repeated, whereas the larger part of the remainder would seem to be nonexistent. Some musicians are so embittered by this fact, by the "injustice" of the world, that they never manage to get over it. A respected composer once said to me: "I have made a name for myself. If I write a new piece of orchestral music it will appear on the programme of all German philharmonic societies tomorrow. But there it rests. Obviously they sit quietly waiting for me to write a new piece very year. But how am I to manage to secure a second or third performance?"

One could go on to ask, why are Strauss's *Till Eulenspiegel*, Debussy's *La Mer*, Strawinsky's *Petrouchka* performed again and again? How have Bach and Beethoven always managed to keep their names on the programmes?

There are people who say: if other works were as popular and as well-known as those mentioned, they would be just as important. But why is it that they fail to become popular? Surely there must be a reason for it.

Above all there must be a reason why audiences have maintained an attitude of hostility towards most contemporary music for upwards of forty years, and why this hostility, this chasm within musical life, has not grown less in the course of time, despite all the endeavours of musicians and the press to enlighten our audiences. Let no-one say that this has always been the case. Many masterpieces were misunderstood at first, it is true, because the audience was unaccustomed to the idiom, or because it was a bad performance. But such a state of affairs never lasted; sooner or later they became recognised for what they were. The tension which gradually grew up between musicians and audiences owing to the latter's lack of appreciation of these masterpieces was always relaxed again. But today things are different. This state of latent tension has been in existence now for more than a generation. If you will not acknowledge a crisis in music or musicians you must at least acknowledge a crisis in audiences. And is not the latter even worse than the former?

As a conductor I am familiar with the reaction of audiences. The modern musician, to put it plainly, must hold his own against Mozart and Beethoven in the concert hall. The theory according to which new and old music are diametrically and irreconcilably opposed is a hypothesis postulated by convinced reactionaries and super-progressives alike for the purpose of preventing any discussion between the two, or between them and the public. But it is precisely this which is essential. No work can escape being contrasted and compared with other works. It is frequently found that new works which make a great impression at a festival of contemporary music later lose most of their effect in ordinary concert routine, when they have to compete with the classics and with other music. But this and this alone is after all the tribunal before which even new works must hold their own in the long run. Music and musical life are indivisible, and we cannot pretend that the past through which we have all lived does not exist and never did exist.

But it is this very circumstance which makes the position of the modern composer so difficult, as compared with that of the modern painter or sculptor. The latter are never at a loss for occasions calling for the exercise of their art: there are always public squares crying out for statues and private houses clamouring for works of art. The art of the past had its own particular task; as far as modern life is concerned, the modern artist's path is never barred by the art or the artists of any bygone age.

But if the composer of today is to fulfil any practical purpose at all, if he wishes his works to be performed, he must be prepared to share his place in the sun with all his predecessors, back to medieval times, since it is customary, in our philharmonic societies, to allow all known musical works to be heard in the limited number of concerts arranged by them. The composer of today is indeed faced with overpowering competition, and he is the victim of a merciless system of selection. Those against whom he must measure himself, who usurp his position, are the greatest masters in the history of music, the heirs of eras of fecundity, the idolised favourites of the public. He must justify his existence and prove his worth anew every day in the face of the greatest masterpieces of the past. If he does not pass the test he is heard no more and must resign his claim.

In view of this situation, which can only be called critical, it is hardly surprising that in more recent times composers began to band together, to form groups and parties which had their attendant peculiarities and advantages and also their ridiculous oddities. Art is not after all an affair for the masses; if anything, it is a matter of the highest responsibility on the part of the individual, and it must therefore strike us as not without humour that geniuses should suddenly crop up by the dozen, when there have never been more than a very few great artists at any one time in the past. This is to a very large extent the fault of the press, which has become an energetic champion of the cause of modern music. In the past, let us say in the nineteenth century, experts and critics were rather averse to modern music; if it won through at all it did so in spite of all opposition. Today it is awarded laurels as it were in advance, but then cases of real "winning through" in the earlier sense of the term have become all the rarer.

As I have mentioned above, the characteristic feature of the situation, i.e. the profound distrust which audiences feel for serious contemporary music, has been in existence for a long time—roughly since the first world war. Two conclusions can be drawn from this: firstly, that in spite of the fact that such a long time has passed, modern music has failed to overcome this general distrust, or to appeal to a larger public (the few exceptions to this only prove the rule). And secondly, that this distrust and hostility did not succeed on the other hand in seriously endangering the so-called new music, or in making its existence impossible. It cannot be denied that it exists, and that it has come to stay. It is a reality, and none the less so if it manifests itself, as some people think, more in formulas and designs evolved by theoreticians than in great achievements. However that may be, it has and holds a limited but passionately devoted public.

Now we have to agree that this tension has been in existence for 40 years. And during these 40 years no solution has been found, although the problem has occupied many a good brain and many a great talent. Let us therefore attempt to clear things up by examining the music itself.

We find that a fundamental change in the tonal material on which music is based announced itself as early as the turn of the century. Arnold Schoenberg was the man who gave the decisive momentum to that movement among musicians with the aim of superseding the system of major and minor keys which until then had reigned supreme. Schoenberg's followers—whose numbers were increased as time went on by modern musicians all over the world—maintained that the system on which the development of European music since the Renaissance and the baroque period had been based was obsolete. "Atonal" music, as it has generally been called since, was born under the sign of progress; people desired above all else something new. Now the clamour for something new, the theoretical demand for a forcing of progress at any price, was, in the manner in which it was raised in the first place and has continued ever since, in itself something new. Thus for the first time the substance itself, the stuff of which music is made, the sound and harmonies of which it is composed, became the starting-point and not as in the past, man, who changes with the course of history and makes use of this substance, impressing his stamp upon it. A particular example quoted in this connection was Wagner's *Tristan*, which was supposed to have expanded and developed chromatic harmonies with a consistency unknown in the history of music until that date. This theory leaves out of consideration, of course, the fact that in writing *Tristan*, Wagner had no intention at all of creating something "new", of "expanding" the laws of harmony, of "forcing" progress, but was solely and exclusively concerned with finding the most adequate and impressive language for his poetic vision, for his "Tristan" world. This is proved not only by every bar of *Tristan*, but also in another sense by the works which he wrote after *Tristan* and which represent without exception more or less serious "falls from grace" in the eyes of the believers in progress. Like all his predecessors, Wagner was only concerned about finding adequate expression for the spiritual world he wanted to portray. The fact that in so doing he discovered the chromatic system which was of such significance for the future, was far from essential as far as he was concerned; it was a mere accident.

To derive development from the substance and not from the human being searching for expression, to seek and to postulate not the "beautiful" but the "new"; this, as I have mentioned above, is the great novelty which was introduced into the history of music at the turn of the century. And if we are to understand the subsequent course of this development we must follow for a distance the way of thought by which it moved and the mental processes underlying it. Let us then examine the stuff itself and try to be quite clear as to just what modern atonality is. To this end we must know what tonality is and what it is that differentiates the two.

The cadence is the basis of tonality, i.e. of the expression of music within the scope of definite keys. It is the cadence which "determines" the key. Its simplest progression, via the upper dominant to the lower dominant and then back to the tonic, covers a certain definite ground. This not only means that in such a progression each chord is connected with its neighbour, i.e. with the preceding or the following chord, but—and this is the decisive point—a context is created on a higher plane, which connects all the links of the chain with each other from the starting point to the end. By means of this super-imposed relationship, this "area" marked out by the cadence, no less than the decisive factor is achieved: music can take shape. It has found a point of departure, a course to run, a goal to attain. Thus a definiteness was introduced into the world of sound which had previously been lacking, an element so powerful, of such compelling attraction that one can hardly picture today, and it is quite understandable, how men strove for hundreds of years broadly speaking, step by step to master it.

From tentative beginnings they developed unceasingly and according to its own laws—as with every true natural process, for such is what it is—that system of tonality in musical thinking and feeling which was to become the complete and exclusive possession of European humanity. That we are dealing here with one of the great forces of Nature is proved, for one thing, by the fact that it is accepted by people when they start to sing together, or by children (musical prodigies), or by remote races, such as the Japanese, who previously knew nothing about it, with the same compulsion as it is by us. It is manifest, moreover, in the simplest as well as in the most complex musical works. Its omnipotence applies to the smallest no less than to the largest. Strictly tonal music can indeed be described as a closed series of "cadences". A Bach fugue or a movement of a Beethoven symphony—such as the first movement of the ninth symphony—literally represents a cadence on a gigantic scale.

At the beginning of this century, the Viennese musician Hauer made the "discovery" that Beethoven had really been writing nothing but cadences all his life. In the spirit of the age that prompted such a "discovery" he thought that he had thereby found the key to the final explanation of Beethoven's music, had administered to it the *coup de grâce*. "Nothing but cadences"—as if that had any bearing on the meaning of Beethoven's music. It is just like saying that, in the last analysis, Caesar and Bismarck consisted of "nothing but" water or oxygen. It takes a lot of obtuseness and a great lack of imagination to pride oneself, as Hauer did, on this "discovery".

The principle of tonality occupies a dominating position even where it is not, as in the classical composers, applied rigorously to the structure of the whole composition. It cements as it were the individual bricks together; tonality is involved whenever the succession of individual chords is integrated into a larger whole. Thus, a tonal work looks rather like the sea: big waves carrying small waves, and small waves smaller waves still, etc. In this simile, waves correspond to cadence spans—a multiplicity of ever smaller cadence spans superimposed upon one another. We are therefore dealing with a system of separate forces running their course independently of our intentions or wishes. It is not until our will of expression coincides and unites with the will of expression of these forces that the work of art is born. And this is the sole reason why it receives once and for all the unalterable character peculiar to it which makes it equally effective for all people at all times, as has been proved by the great European musical masterpieces for several centuries.

The extent of the tonality of a work can be determined with a very high degree of accuracy. In Wagner's *Tristan*, for example, which is so often put forward as the principal witness for musical progress, every single note must be considered as tonal in the strict sense of the word. This applies also to Strauss, to Debussy, and to the early work of Strawinsky. But whereas it is extremely easy to define the domain of tonality, it is by no means so easy to say where chromaticism, polytonality, atonality or whatever you wish to call it really starts. The theoreticians disagree on this point. Hindemith would discover the beginnings of atonality not only in Wagner's *Tristan*, but even in Mozart, a contention which is easily confuted. In his own work, as in that of Strawinsky, Bartók and others, tonality recurs in a greater or lesser degree. It is only natural that the champions of atonality should endeavour to prove that it developed from tonality, as the logical consequence of tendencies implicit in tonality. But it cannot be denied that these attempts are ill-founded. It must be admitted that consistent atonality was something completely new. It is important to realise that atonality does not constitute the final result of the evolution of tonality, but that it is something which really had not existed before in this particular form. This becomes apparent the moment we examine the principles of form of the atonal composer. Hindemith says the following about the so-called twelve-tone system:

> "Nowhere does Nature offer a hint that it would be desirable to play a definite number of notes within a definite compass in a definite period of time. It is possible to find any number of such arbitrarily formulated regulations, and if styles of composition were to be based upon them I could imagine more extensive and more interesting rules of the game. To limit musical composition to a set system of combinations of sound seems to me more doctrinaire than the postulates of out-and-out diatonic theoreticians."

The question of why such a system was, or had to be, created is perhaps even more interesting than the twelve-tone technique itself. It certainly seems as though up to now atonality has lacked a uniform theoretical foundation. There is a clash of widely divergent opinions. Hindemith's serious and detailed attempt at explanation was not left uncontradicted. Strawinsky thought that theory ought to follow practice: the time for it had not yet arrived. The only important thing was to recognise that the system of tonality had really been expanded and superseded. On the other hand the twelve-tone system represents an attempt to impose upon the material of the atonal musician form, structure, and consistency as it were from outside. This implies that intrinsic form, structure, and consistency are lacking, at any rate in the sense in which the material of the tonal musician, based as it is on the cadence interval, i.e. on a law of Nature, would seem to possess them.

We are dealing with art. But art is, first and last, a form of human expression. And if the material of art refuses to yield an answer, we must turn to the man in whose hands it is after all nothing more than a means to an end. In my opinion we are therefore justified in asking: to what extent does the tonal or atonal material of music correspond to the organic biological constitution of man?

On this subject the history of European music through the centuries has something to tell us. And we find that it was tonality and tonality alone which enabled music to achieve a degree of independence it had never before possessed in the history of man.

Music is realised in the dimension of time. The cadence of the tonal system makes it possible for a two-dimensional musical progression from one note to the next to be subordinated to an all-embracing unity on a higher plane, and thus to acquire a third dimension which was unknown to it before. It is by no means misleading to draw a comparison, as Spengler did, between tonality in this sense and the discovery of perspective. Its position with regard to the dimension of time (in which music finds realisation) is the same as that of the third dimension, depth, with regard to the plastic arts. Both tonality and perspective owe their discovery to one and the same view of life, although music was not fully developed until a later date. However that may be, a Bach fugue, a classical symphony possess, as forms, such a high degree of sovereign independence that nothing in the literature of music can bear anything like a comparison with them. This "abstract" music does not merely reflect the events of life, is not merely occasioned by them, as all music had been in the past. It is not mere "utilitarian" music, bound up with life and incorporated into it, mere church music, or dance music, etc. It is not tied to the ballet, to the stage, although it can serve them if it so desires. Whatever it touches, it changes. It embraces the whole fullness of organic life and reflects a vast world of independent forms—the song, the fugue, the sonata are but fundamental types. It can do all this because it is self-sufficient. It is in deep accord with the biological constitution of human nature.

What is this biological constitution?

First of all it contains the problem of tension and relaxation. All organic life existing in time—and music is an art which has its being in time—is subject to the alternation between tension and relaxation. The fluctuation between these two, tension and relaxation, represents the rhythm of life; there is not a moment as long as we breathe, in which one or the other does not prevail. Both are organically connected. Of the two states, the second, the state of relaxation, is the one which comes first, if we want to put it that way, the more "original" state. It is one of the fundamental doctrines of modern biology that it is *relaxation* which plays the decisive part, for instance, in many complicated physical functions (singing, playing musical instruments like the violin, or the piano, even riding, skiing, etc.). It is, moreover, a state which appears to the modern European (and this applies also to the modern American) to be somewhat difficult to attain. It is somewhat alien to the character of our civilisation, since this sets so much store by the tension of energies. And for that very reason it is the more significant. This relaxation, which precedes all tension and which alone endows all kinds of tension with possibilities and scope, is found within the sphere of music—and this must be stated absolutely unequivocally—only in tonality. Tonality alone is able to represent it as *objectively existing* (anything and everything can of course be stated subjectively, in the guise of a personal mood) because it has at its disposal the archetypal combination of sounds, the major common chord. This triad has two properties which constitute relaxation:

1. It is a beginning or an end, which means that a kind of definition of locality is implicit in it (we shall examine later what is the biological significance of this definition of locality). It is not therefore a transition.

2. It is self-sufficient. It can therefore be sustained indefinitely. The opening passages of certain symphonic works (such as the beginning of Anton Bruckner's romantic

symphony with its sustained E flat major chord) represent the archetype of the degree of relaxation of which music is capable.

Now it is upon the firm basis of this triad that, in tonal music, the cadence is erected. Tension grows out of relaxation to embrace life in all its variety, to return at last, in accordance with the law which called it into being, to the point from which it started, to the so-called tonic. Tension and relaxation are mutually dependent to a very high degree. The more profound, the more complete the relaxation, the greater will be the tensions based upon it. We can even go so far as to say that no tension could be created or relaxed without a corresponding state of relaxation which must precede it. Therefore, for all its excitement (which can be carried to the limits of human understanding) every masterpiece of tonal music radiates a profound, unshakable, penetrating peace—a reflection, as it were, of the glory of God.

It is this "tranquility in the midst of motion", as one feels tempted to define it—a peculiar characteristic of music informed by tonality—which is lacking in non-tonal music. In place of the tension of cadence that can hold big passages together are substituted other tensions of a smaller, even of a minute kind. A multiplicity of movement without objective, a deep restlessness, have taken such music in their grip. Pauses, which are of course inevitable in the domain of changing rhythms, are few and far between, and appear to be the expression of subjective "moods" rather than moments of relaxation with an objective reality of their own and a predetermined place within the whole. Where music lacks the comprehensive tensions and connecting forms of tonality, these little tensions from note to note must supply the want. Admittedly, they are always at work, but they are more than ever inevitable in non-tonal music. The continuous mechanical rhythm which makes it appear as though many of these pieces have more in common with a lifeless, spiritually immobile machine than with living man does, it is true, completely occupy the mind of the listener for the time being. But when it is over one asks oneself what one has really heard: the full synthesis, the meaning of the whole, is all too often not apparent. It is sometimes astonishing what wealth of intelligence is to be found in the permutations and combinations of atonal music; as an achievement of the intellect it can in certain circumstances rank extremely high. But the price it must pay for this from the biological point of view is a lack of the vital values.

A further characteristic peculiar to music based on tonality is its geographical logic. I have already pointed out that it is in the nature of the cadence to follow a certain route, that it creates the possibility of a beginning, i.e. a starting-point, and an end, i.e. a finishing-point. But this means that the listener, in a work which is really completely impregnated with tonality—and this is not by any means the case with all music composed during the period of pure tonality—always knows where he is, throughout the journey, and that this assurance of orientation is never once dimmed in the whole course of the piece. Such an achievement is highly characteristic of tonality, and it becomes particularly astounding when it embraces the largest of musical forms, like long movements of a symphony (e.g. Beethoven's ninth symphony, first movement). It is this characteristic which endows tonal music with that precision which belongs to it alone, and which makes it really independent in the last analysis of all external images, and of any imitation of the objective world.

This characteristic, too, has a definite biological value. The feeling for locality, the desire to establish one's position in relation to the surrounding country for the purpose of orientation, i.e. the desire to "know" where one is and where one is going, constitutes one of the earliest instincts of organic life to be developed in man and beast alike. But music which would dispense with tonality is unequal to the task of doing justice to this instinct. Except when describing the world of objects or serving the purposes of choreography or poetry—all so-called programme music is the offspring of biologically weakened periods of creation—it loses quite a considerable part of its precision and definition of utterance. Since its system of tensions and of points of reference is applied from note to note, within a narrowly circumscribed sphere—since it dispenses with the wider tensions, which belong to the domain of the tonal cadence —it takes its bearings from its immediate surroundings. Therefore, if we let ourselves be guided by the atonal musician we walk as it were through a dense forest. The strangest flowers and plants attract our attention by the side of the path. But we do not know where we are going nor whence we have come. The listener is seized by a feeling of being lost, of being at the mercy of the forces of primeval existence. It seems as though the atonal musician had not paid much attention to the listener as an independent personality: the listener is faced with an all-powerful world of chaos. But of course it must be admitted that this strikes a certain chord in the apprehensions of modern man!

Once again it can be seen that the price paid for this wealth, this freedom, this chaotic mystery of atonality is a lack of a biological, vital character, it is this and nothing else that we called lack of orientation. We cannot escape from the conclusion that a type of music which dispenses with a device to regulate tension and relaxation, thereby sacrificing the geographical precision of tonality (whatever other qualities it might acquire in the process), must be considered as *biologically inferior*. It does not depict forces running their course. This biological inferiority may be balanced by intellectual superiority, but this does not change the facts of the case. It is this element of biological insufficiency implicit in the substance of atonal music, an

unavoidable element for the atonal musician, which is at
the root of the insuperable, stubborn opposition offered to
this kind of music by the vast majority of the public. This
antipathy will affect anyone who is not instinctively prepared to sacrifice his biological balance to the sensations
and considerations of intellectual individualism. In other
words, it will affect the majority of those persons, even
today, who combine to make up what is called the "general" public.

But this inevitably leads to the question of why, if that is
the case, atonal music has not disappeared long since?
Why is it that it maintains its position in spite of everything? It is, after all, well over 40 years old by now and yet
there are no indications that the arguments and postulates
it introduced have lost their force.

There is a reason for every phenomenon: otherwise it
would not exist. Atonal music would never have been in-
vented, if something in modern man had not required it.
Similar phenomena can be observed in other sphers of art.
Admittedly, the concept of atonal music is due to a large
extent to the idea of progress for its own sake and to the
unchecked proliferation of material which is its result. And
yet, unless atonality had somehow assisted the need for self
expression of modern man, unless it had corresponded
somehow with his *awareness of the world*, he would never
have made it his own.

I am fully aware of the onesidedness of the following
remarks: they represent one explanation only of a complex
set of facts.

The greatest revolution in this awareness of the world
during the history of European civilisation proceeds from
the discovery made by Copernicus. It is only in this present
age that we are becoming alive to the full implications of
the unparalleled revolution which occurred in the thought
of man when it was realised that the earth was not, as
Ptolemy held, the centre of the known universe, but moved

around the sun—in other words, that some power transcending that of humanity was at work in the universe. All the previous cultural achievements of mankind in Europe right up to Christianity, had been based on the assumption, accepted as a matter of course, that Man was the measure and the centre of things. Notwithstanding the fact that modern science, even to the atom bomb, is based on the discovery made by Copernicus, the anthropomorphic attitude which characterised Ptolemy's view of the world has remained in force, unchallenged, in the realms of art and culture. Not only is the art of antiquity and that last flower of the culture of antiquity, Christianity, absolutely convinced of the decisive importance of the human being, of the immortal soul of each individual, but all the art of more recent periods, down to modern times, takes it for granted. The two views of the world are in the last analysis diametrically opposed to one another: the ptolemaic-Christian view, according to which the universe in the true sense revolves around Man, whom God created in His image and for whom Christ died, and the Copernican view, which considers Man as nothing more than a speck of dust within a huge universe which is beyond the scope of human measurements and concepts. In spite of this, people held both these views simultaneously for many centuries without giving the matter much thought. It is understandable that a poet like Goethe should apply even to Nature the view according to which man is the centre and measure of things, but Kant, too, who was quite different in every other respect, seems to have found it perfectly natural to hold these basically irreconcilable views, somewhat naïvely, in speaking of the law of the universe beyond man and of the moral law within him. Nietzsche was the first to realise to the full the disastrous contradiction involved in this state of affairs. He, too, was the first to draw the dreadful consequences which his age demanded more and more urgently to be drawn or at least theoretically explored. Nietzsche tasted the full bitterness of the problem, without finally getting—through a "genealogy of morals"—any further than a blind "will to power" as the final motive force. It was a mere formula, a principle beyond all ethics and all personal human responsibility, which may have corresponded to the reality of the superhuman and non-human universe, but which left out of consideration the reality of Man as an individual—as if the latter were not a "reality" also, an exactly and biologically determinable reality. We are all witnesses of the effects, past and present, of this principle of Nietzsche's in history, through two world crises down to the atom bomb.

Although one might hesitate to equate such a cold abstraction (with which mankind seems to have arrived at the point of being able to lift itself off its own hinges) with the abstract principles of atonal music, it must at least be admitted that the principle of tonality, in which each note is referred to the whole range of human emotion, and man, as listener, is unreservedly made the centre of the whole, corresponds to the anthropomorphic, ptolemaic-Christian view of the world. Tonality is as it were a late child of this view of the world, and the masterpieces of tonal music have become the last and sweetest flower of the creative cultural genius of Europe.

Tonality appears to us in all respects to be a law of nature, howbeit a law of nature which "holds sway" within the human soul and its emotions. This is the reason why all attempts to give an exact physical definition of all the forces liberated during the performance of a "tonal" work have been unsuccessful. Many men, from Helmholz down to Hindemith, have attempted to formulate these strange laws, to define them, to relate them somehow to physical facts, to explain physically in terms of frequency of oscillations, harmonics, and so on, things of which the explanation really lies in the domain of the human soul. But always in vain. The balance can never be struck. The laws according to which a Beethoven sonata movement is constructed, are laws of the human soul, of organic life. They are basically, and *in principle* different from those governing physics and astronomy. The substance of music, arranged according to the laws of tonality, manifests *biological* facts, not physical or cosmic facts.

But although these laws cannot be "objectively" observed, they are laws none the less. Even if they cannot be calculated scientifically or circumscribed in terms of figures and mathematical formulae, they are still part of a natural process following an ordained law—still part of Nature. Because, however, they belong to organic life, their myriad complexities make them extraordinary difficult to recognise as *laws*: considerably more difficult than all the calculable technicalities of the "machine" which the intelligence of man has constructed.

When I speak of tonality and atonality as two opposed principles, I do so purely in terms of ideas. In practice, the dividing line between tonality and atonality is rarely so clearly defined. The world of tonality is, by its nature, clearly defined. The boundaries can be extended, but they cannot fluctuate. From the "tonal" point of view, it is clear where tonality ends and atonality begins. From the "atonal" point of view it is less clear. Atonality appears at its purest in the work of the man who first enabled it to break through, Arnold Schoenberg. It flourished in the period after the first world war. That was the time when it saw the light as a new discovery, as it were, and when great hopes were founded upon it. Today, after the second world war, we seem to be passing through similar times. But the situation has changed. Such leading composers as, above all, Strawinsky, Hindemith, Bartók, and others, have since experienced a partial conversion to tonality. However that may be, the co-existence of both tendencies is, of course, nothing more than a faithful reflection of the human spirit today, which would fain exchange the narrow garden of what is merely human (tonality) for the dread liberty of cosmic space, although it feels that it is thus endangering its biological organical nature.

One last question: to which of these two principles does the future belong? Which will emerge victorious from the struggle which has now lasted 40 years? I am not of the opinion—frequently held by people nervous at the errors of judgment made in the history of music—that we cannot and ought not to make up our minds about contemporary artists and contemporary art, to appreciate or condemn them. But this battle of the worlds would never have been joined if there had not been genuine reasons behind it. Wherever it is really at work, the power of tonality remains unbroken. On the other hand the problems first posed by atonal music have lost none of their force. Every design to make history or to forestall the decisions of history is foolish. All we can say is that force will be of no avail in compelling a decision which must be allowed to mature in peace if it is to be of any value at all. Neither the attempts of atonal fanatics to exert some sort of spiritual pressure by their publications nor the edicts of authoritarian states can settle a question the answer to which can and must come from the innermost recesses of human nature, i.e. in concrete, musical terms, from the "public".

Faced with the turmoil of the modern scene—of which the turmoil in the sphere of music is merely the reflection—the Christian may well speak of the inscrutable ways of God. He will bow his head in humility before this inscrutability, it may even appear to him as a new source of adoration.

In the words of Goethe:

> „Wenn im Unendlichen dasselbe
> Sich wiederholend ewig fliesst,
> Das tausendfaltige Gewolbe
> Sich kräftig ineinanderschliesst,

Stromt Lebenslust aus allen Dingen
Dem grössten wie dem kleinsten Stern
Und alles Drangen, alles Ringen
Ist ewige Ruh in Gott dem Herrn."
(When in infinity the Same
repeated flows eternally
and when the thousandfold domain
is firmly joined together
the joy of life flows from all things
the smallest and the largest star
and all the surgings, all the strugglings,
are laid to rest in God the Lord.)